Table of Contents

Yggdrasil Plug-and-Play Linux

The Yggdrasil Linux/GNU/X-Windows Operating System
Fall 1995, Revision A
For ISA, EISA, VLB or PCI-based PC Compatibles
Includes complete source code!

- Linux 1.2.13 kernel supporting most popular CD-ROM drives (see hardware list on back).
- An easy install script, plus a graphical interface for system configuration.
- *The X Window System:* X11R6 XFree86 3.1.2 (see hardware list on back), Xlib/Xt X windows libraries, the Tcl/Tk programming language and toolkit, and the Xview 3.2 OpenLook(tm) toolkit.
- The Andrew System version 6.3.3, including the `ez` editor for easy creation and reading of documents with imbedded images, equations, spreadsheets, hypertext links, and many other media types.
- *Ethernet Networking* with TCP/IP, RPC and other Internet protocols.
- Games: asteroids, battle zone, chess, mille bornes, othello, pool, shogi, solitaire, tetris, and connect four.
- *Multimedia:* viewers for JPEG, GIF, TIFF and other image formats, MPEG video, support for many sound cards.
- *Text editors:* the elvis vi clone, GNU Emacs, and X-Emacs.
- *Desktop Publishing:* TEX, LaTeX and groff typesetting packages with X previewers, and ghostscript, a postscript interpreter for X windows, faxes and a variety of printers.
- *Telecommunications:* Z-modem, Taylor UUCP, mail readers, threaded USENET news reader with support for reading MIME multimedia messages with imbedded images, full motion video and sound.
- The Postgres95 0.02-beta remote database system.
- *Programming Languages:* GNU C++, GNU ANSI C FORTRAN-to-C and Pascal-to-C translators.
- *Enhanced development environment:* GNU debugger, bison, flex, GNU make, Revision Controls System, Concurrent Version System, GNATS, and Berkeley yacc.
- System V-style shared memory and interprocess communication.
- *File Systems:* an advanced filesystem with long file names, symbolic links, and FIFOs. A process filesystem (/proc), System V, Xenix, Coherent, Minix, NFS, DOS, HPFS (read-only), and ISO-9660/Rock-Ridge CD-ROM filesystems.
- *Emulators:* a BIOS emulator that can run DOS, an ELF loader, and a snapshot of an MS-Windows emulator under development.

1 Introduction

This manual will guide you through the installation of Yggdrasil Plug and Play Linux and introduce you to the on-line documentation. It is not meant to be a tutorial on how to use Linux and will often refer you to on-line manual pages and info sections. At the root of this is the sheer magnitude of the distribution package; thousands of programs come with Plug and Play Linux. Many of them come with special instructions, and entire books have been written about others. In fact, one program included in Plug and Play Linux has more than 800 pages in two volumes written about one part of it.

The third edition of the Linux Bible, at nearly 1600 pages, is the single most comprehensive volume on Linux, but even it is unable to cover everything included in Plug and Play Linux. The Linux Bible is a must for new Linux users as well as Linux veterans who realize the value of hard copy documentation. The Linux Bible is published by Yggdrasil Computing and contains *Linux Installation and Getting Started*, *The Linux Network Administrators' Guide*, *The Linux Users' Guide*, *The Kernel Hackers Guide*, and more than 30 Howto Guides. Please see the order form at the end of this manual for more information on ordering.

Although even this volume of documentation is unable to completely describe a package as rich as Plug and Play Linux, in most cases you can begin exploring without the help of any manual at all, including this one. The system is designed so that putting the CD-ROM in the drive and booting from the boot floppy is enough for you to be running a Linux system. If you happen to have a system incorporating unsupported hardware, it is still possible to install Plug and Play Linux entirely from within DOS, so that only your hard drive and processor need to be supported in order to get up and running.

With this manual you should have received a copy of the Fall 1995 Plug and Play Linux CD-ROM, the Fall 1995 Plug and Play Linux Source Code CD-ROM, and a boot floppy. If you have not received all these items, please return the book to the store where it was purchased and request a new, complete copy.

Most of the screen snapshots in this manual represent how the image will appear on a monochrome terminal. On the Linux console, these screens will look much nicer. The content remains the same.

2 Installation of the Base System

Plug and Play Linux is designed to install with as little intervention from the user as possible. So, armed with a little knowledge of disk partitioning, some free space on your hard drive, and a spirit of adventure, you will be able to install Plug and Play Linux with little recourse to this manual. If you need some help partitioning your hard drive or if some of your system's hardware is not properly detected during the install process, then this chapter will be useful. If you wish to have someone walk you through the installation, than please Section 8.5.1 [900 number], page 80.

2.1 Getting Started

There are two ways to install Plug-and-Play Linux from CDROM:

- If you have a supported hardware configuration, you should be able to put the system CD and boot floppy in your CDROM drive, turn the power on, and you will be running Linux (which is what this chapter discusses). Some additional hardware platforms are supported with special boot floppies.
- Otherwise, you can use an experimental install from DOS-based installation (See Section 2.7.2 [dos install], page 23).

Begin by placing the Plug and Play Linux CD in your CD-ROM drive. If you are running DOS, you should be able to run `dir` on the CD and see the files. Under DOS, the files on the CD will appear to have funny names; this is because the disk uses the Rock Ridge extensions to get the full benefits of a Linux file system. DOS is limited to the file names you see. To help you access the Plug and Play CD under DOS, we have included a file '`TRANS.TBL`' in each directory which gives the real names of each of the files as well as their DOS names. If you think that your CD may have been damaged during shipping or if you are just curious, you should explore the CD under DOS and see if you can read all the files. If DOS has no problems with the CD, then you can install Plug and Play Linux under DOS (See Section 2.7.2 [dos install], page 23), although this is not the preferred method. Please try to install from within Linux first as you system will be faster and more reliable if you do.

After putting the Plug and Play Linux CD in the drive, put the included boot floppy in your floppy drive, and boot from it. If you need a 5.25 inch boot floppy, you can receive one at no charge by calling Yggdrasil Computing at +1-408-261-6630 or you can create one yourself under DOS by putting the Plug and Play Linux CD in your CD-ROM drive, a blank floppy in your '`A:`' drive and running the program `\dosbin\mkfloppy` on the CD. So if your CD-ROM drive is '`E:`' you would type

```
e:
cd \dosbin
mkfloppy
```

This same command will work for making a new 3.5 inch boot floppy, should you ever need one. You can make a boot floppy on your 'b:' drive by typing `mkfloppy b:`.

In addition, `mkfloppy` can be used to create a number of other special boot floppies for other circumstances:

default This is the boot floppy that came with your copy of Plug-and-Play Linux.

network This is a boot floppy that can be used to install another machine over ethernet or a SLIP line.

noscsi This is a boot floppy with all SCSI drivers removed. Sometimes the process of checking for a SCSI device can cause certain systems to hang. So this stripped down boot floppy is provided.

pcmcia
pcmcia2 Boot floppies for using PCMCIA bus notebook computers.

Once you have the proper boot floppy, put it in your boot drive (normally drive 'a:') and boot from it. Note that some computers are set to always boot from the hard drive. With these computers it is necessary to tell them specifically to boot from the floppy. This is normally accomplished by altering the CMOS configuration. If you have this problem, please consult the manuals that came with your computer.

When you reset your computer, you should see something like

```
 ----------------------------------------------------------------
|                                                                |
| System Configuration (C) Copyright 1985-1991, Megatrends Inc., |
|________________________________________________________________|
| Main Processor : 80486            | Base Memory Size : 640 KB  |
| Numeric Processor : Present       | Ext. Memory Size : 7424 KB |
| Floppy Drive A: : 1.2MB, 5.25''   | Hard disk C: type : None   |
| Floppy Drive B: : None            | Hard disk D: type : None   |
| Display Type: VGA/PGA/EGA         | Serial Port(s): 3F8        |
| ROM BIOS Date:  07/07/91          | Parallel Ports(s) : 378    |
|___________________________________|____________________________|

256KB CACHE MEMORY

LDLINUX.SYS 1.20 07/27/95 Copyright (c) 1994-95 H. Peter Anvin
```

What you actually see will depend on your particular hardware, so don't be concerned if what you see is different from the above. The only line which should not depend on your hardware is

```
LDLINUX.SYS 1.20 07/27/95 Copyright (c) 1994-95 H. Peter Anvin
```

This line tells you that SYSLINUX has loaded and is preparing to load Linux. After a few seconds, the screen should fill with text and you should see the '`boot:`' prompt. At this point your screen should show

```
~~~~      ~~~~     ~~~~~    ~~~~~~~~~~    Plug-and-Play Linux Fall 1995
   ~~    ~~      ~~     ~       ~~        Yggdrasil Computing, Incorporated
    ~~  ~~      ~~        ~     ~~        http://www.yggdrasil.com
     ~~~~      ~~               ~~        ftp://ftp.yggdrasil.com/pub/fall95
      ~~       ~~               ~~
      ~~       ~~               ~~        General Linux Consulting:
      ~~        ~~        ~     ~~        1-900-446-6075 ext. 835 ("TEK")
      ~~         ~~      ~      ~~        $2.95/minute, USA only
      ~~          ~~    ~       ~~        11am-noon,1pm-5pm Pacific
     ~~~~          ~~~~~~   ~~~~~~~~~~    Outside the USA +1 408 261 6630
   /  ||  \                               (billed to credit card)

Press ENTER to load Yggdrasil Plug-and-Play Linux, or enter "linux"
followed by any boot-time parameters you might need now.  You will
have to enter boot-time parameters if your hardware is not properly
detected automatically.  If you do not have a Panasonic/Matsushita,
IBM, Creative Labs or TEAC CD-ROM, you probably want to enter "sbpcd=0".

For information on boot-time options:

Press F1 for general options     Press F4 for non-SCSI, non-IDE CD-ROMS
Press F2 for SCSI options        Press F5 for floppy disk options
Press F3 for IDE options

boot: _
```

Unless you are certain your hardware will not be detected properly, you should not type anything here. Instead wait 10 seconds for Linux to start loading. If you know your hardware will not be properly detected please see Chapter 3 [boot prompt], page 25 for information on what you can do to try to force hardware detection. If you do accidentally type something here, use the `<-` key to back space over it and then press **ENTER**. SYSLINUX will then continue the default booting procedure.

As SYSLINUX loads Linux, it will display the word "Loading" followed by a number of dots, so you should see something like

```
Loading........
```

The exact number of dots depends on the size of the Linux kernel which is being loaded. After a few moments, the kernel will have loaded and it will start probing for hardware. As each driver locates hardware which it controls, a message is displayed. Unfortunately, many drivers display messages even when they do not detect the appropriate hardware, so do not be worried if you see error messages related to hardware which is not a part of your computer. As the system boots, you should see a display which looks something like

```
Console: color EGA+ 80x25, 1 virtual console (max 63)
Kernel arguments: auto BOOT_IMAGE=linux ramdisk=1440
bios32_init : BIOS32 Service Directory structure at 0x000fc4e0
bios32_init : BIOS32 Service Directory entry at 0xfc8c0
pcibios_init : PCI BIOS revision 2.00 entry at 0xfc8f0 Probing PCI hardware.
Calibrating delay loop.. ok - 30.22 BogoMips
Serial driver version 4.11 with no serial options enabled tty00 at 0x03f8
(irq = 4) is a 16550A
tty01 at 0x02f8 (irq = 3) is a 16550A
Logitech Bus mouse detected and installed with IRQ 5.
snd3 <Pro AudioSpectrum 16 rev 127> at 0x388 irq 10 drq 6
snd1 <Yamaha OPL-3 FM> at 0x388 irq 0 drq 0 hda: FX400_02, ATAPI, CDROM drive
ide0: primary interface on irq 14
Floppy drive(s): fd0 is 1.44M
FDC 0 is a 8272A
Configuring Adaptec at IO:330, IRQ 11, DMA priority 5
scsi-ncr53c7,8xx : at PCI bus 0, device 12, function 0
scsi-ncr53c7,8xx : NCR53c810 at memory 0xfbfff000, io 0xe800, irq 12
scsi1 : using io mapped access
scsi1 : using initiator ID 7
scsi1 : using level active interrupts
scsi1 : burst length 8
scsi1 : using 40MHz SCSI clock
scsi1 : NCR code relocated to 0x206768
scsi1 : test 1 started
scsi0 : Adaptec 1542
scsi1 : NCR53c7,8xx (rel 4)
scsi : 2 hosts.
Vendor: TOSHIBA Model: CD-ROM XM-3401TA Rev: 1094 Type: CD-ROM ANSI SCSI
revision: 02
Detected scsi CD-ROM sr0 at scsi0, id 2, lun 0
Vendor: IMS      Model: CDD521/10        Rev: 2.06
Type: WORM      ANSI SCSI revision: 01
Detected scsi CD-ROM sr1 at scsi0, id 3, lun 0
Vendor: SEAGATE Model: ST11900N Rev: 9200
Type: Direct-Access      ANSI SCSI revision: 02
Detected scsi disk sda at scsi1, id 0, lun 0
scsi : detected 2 SCSI cdroms 1 SCSI disk total.
SCSI Hardware sector size is 512 bytes on device sda
Memory: 30956k/32768k available (688k kernel code, 384k reserved, 740k data)
 This processor honors the WP bit even when in supervisor mode. Good.
Swansea University Computer Society NET3.019
Swansea University Computer Society TCP/IP for NET3.019
IP Protocols: ICMP, UDP, TCP
eth0: SMC Ultra at 0x280, 00 00 C0 82 71 B7, IRQ 15 memory 0xd0000-0xd3fff.
smc-ultra.c:v1.12 1/18/95 Donald Becker (becker@cesdis.gsfc.nasa.gov)
Checking 386/387 coupling... Ok, fpu using exception 16 error reporting.
Checking 'hlt' instruction... Ok.
Linux version 1.2.8 (root@adam) (gcc version 2.6.3) #1138 Thu Jun 1 01:03:15
PDT 1995
Partition check:
sda: sda1 sda2 sda3 sda4
```

What you see will differ from this depending on precisely what hardware is detected. This particular machine is unusual in that it has more than one SCSI adapter, as well as an IDE CD-ROM drive. It also displays no error messages about undetected hardware. This is because the kernel of this machine was specially built for it. After you have the system installed, you should do the same by rebuilding your kernel so that the only drivers loaded are for your hardware. This will save memory and shorten the boot process. See Chapter 5 [Recompiling the Kernel], page 35, for information on how to configure a kernel for your particular hardware.

One very important line that the kernel will display as it is booting is the second one:

```
Kernel arguments: auto BOOT_IMAGE=linux ramdisk=1440
```

Notice the last argument to the kernel was "ramdisk=1440". If you do not see a "ramdisk=" argument, or if the argument is "ramdisk=0" then there is a problem. If this occurs you should report the problem to Yggdrasil and reboot. This time at the "boot:" prompt, type

```
boot: linux ramdisk=1440
```

After the partition check, Plug and Play Linux will attempt to mount the Plug and Play Linux CD as root; this is the key step in installing Plug and Play Linux. In fact it really does not matter what kernel you use or where you received it from, any modern kernel which successfully mounts the Plug and Play Linux CD as root and has a ramdisk of at least 1 megabyte, will allow you to install Plug and Play Linux.

If for some reason Linux cannot mount your Plug and Play Linux as root, all is not lost. There are at least two other ways to install Plug and Play Linux, and it may be possible to force Linux to locate your CD-ROM drive. See Chapter 3 [boot prompt], page 25, for information on forcing Linux to detect your hardware, and see Section 2.7 [other install methods], page 23, for information on installing over NFS or from within DOS.

While Plug and Play Linux is attempting to mount your CD-ROM, you may see a number of error reports as the system tests for CD-ROM drives you do not have, or which do not have a CD in them. This is normal.

After the Plug and Play Linux CD has been mounted as root, the ramdisk will be formatted, and some configuration files will be copied into it. After a few moments, you should see the login screen, which looks like

```
~~~~      ~~~~    ~~~~~   ~~~~~~~~~~     Plug-and-Play Linux Fall 1995
   ~~    ~~     ~~     ~      ~~         Yggdrasil Computing, Incorporated
    ~~  ~~    ~~        ~     ~~         http://www.yggdrasil.com
     ~~~~    ~~               ~~         ftp://ftp.yggdrasil.com/pub/fall95
      ~~     ~~               ~~
      ~~     ~~               ~~         General Linux Consulting:
      ~~      ~~        ~     ~~         1-900-446-6075 ext. 835 ("TEK")
      ~~       ~~       ~     ~~         $2.95/minute, USA only
      ~~        ~~     ~      ~~         9AM-5PM Weekdays, Pacific Time
     ~~~~        ~~~~~~   ~~~~~~~~~~
   /  ||  \\


The following user names are automatically installed:

         demo   a demonstration under the X window system.

        guest   an unprivileged user account for exploring the system.

         root   the superuser account for system administration.

      install   install the system on your harddisk

linux login:
```

If you see this screen, then congratulations; you are now running Linux! If you do not get this screen, but instead ultimately get to a message telling you that the system was unable to mount the root floppy, you may want to try the DOS or network based installation system See Section 2.7.2 [dos install], page 23.

If you wish to explore the system, you should log in as the guest user by typing `guest` and pressing the `ENTER` key. The system will be slow as it is running everything off the CD, but everything which is not time dependent will function normally. When you are done exploring the system, type `logout` to return to the login screen.

To see a small fraction of the capabilities of the system, log in as the demo user by typing `demo`. You will then be asked about your video hardware so that the X Window System can be configured. Then the system display should go into graphics mode and the demo will begin.

The most important account that comes pre-configured is the install account. When you log in as `install` the system responds by installing Plug and Play Linux on your hard drive. The rest of this chapter talks about installation using the `install` account.

The install script works best if you leave the boot floppy in the drive. By doing this the script will be able to use the kernel you booted with, which may be different from the one on the CD-ROM e.g. if you have an updated boot floppy. There are also two directories on the boot floppy which may contain special drivers for your hardware, or fixes in the event that there are some bugs in Plug and Play Linux which were not noticed before the CD-ROMs were produced. If you do not leave your boot floppy in the drive, then the install script will not be able to check for any such updates.

The first thing you see when you log in as `install` will be

```
Yggdrasil Computing, Inc.
--------------------------------------------------------------------------
-
    +-------------------------- Keyboards ----------------------------+
    |                                                                 |
    |                                                                 |
    |  You can use the up/down arrow keys to navigate                 |
    |  through the list. Press SPACE to toggle option                 |
    |  on or off.                                                     |
    |                                                                 |
    |  Select your keyboard:                                          |
    | +-------------------------------------------------------------+ |
    | |                   (*) United States                         | |
    | |                   ( ) Belgian                               | |
    | |                   ( ) British                               | |
    | |                   ( ) Danish                                | |
    | |                   ( ) Dvorak                                | |
    | |                   ( ) Emacs                                 | |
    | |                   ( ) Finnish/Swedish                       | |
    | |                   ( ) French                                | |
    +-+----------------------v(+)----------------------------------+-+
    |                    <  OK  >      <Cancel>                       |
    +-----------------------------------------------------------------+
```

This screen allows you to tell Plug and Play Linux what sort of keyboard is attached to your computer. If you just press return, it will assume you have a keyboard with the standard US layout; if you have a different keyboard, then you can select it by moving the cursor up and down with the arrow keys. When you have highlighted the type of keyboard you have, press the `SPACE BAR` to select it. Then press `ENTER`. One keyboard in particular deserves mention; the emacs type is a variation on the US Ascii keyboard intended specifically for hardcore emacs users. It is recommended only for experts.

When you select a keyboard, the keymap will be changed immediately, and the necessary commands will be remembered and later written to the file '`/etc/rc.d/rc.misc/rc.kbd`' so that the proper keyboard type will be selected every time you boot Linux. If you wish to change your keyboard type after you install, simply edit the file '`/etc/rc.d/rc.misc/rc.kbd`'.

After selecting your keyboard type, the next screen you should see is

```
Yggdrasil Computing, Inc.
-----------------------------------------------------------------------------
_




              +---------------- System Name ------------------+
              |                                               |
              |  What would you like to name your system?     |
              |                                               |
              | +-------------------------------------------+ |
              | |linux                                      | |
              | +-------------------------------------------+ |
              +-----------------------------------------------+
              |             <  OK  >      <Cancel>            |
              +-----------------------------------------------+
```

At this point, you are being asked to name your computer. If you computer is not connected to a network in any way, then the name you choose does not matter. If, on the other hand, you expect your computer to be on any sort of network, including one using uucp, then the name you choose becomes important; please consult your local network administrator for information about what name you should choose. If you are on the Internet, you can put your fully qualified domain name here (e.g. linuxbox.mycompany.com).

The name is changed immediately, and also saved so that it may later be written to the file '`/etc/hostname`'; it will be set automatically every time you boot Linux. If you wish to change your hostname at a later date, you can edit the file '`/etc/hostname`', but an easier way is with the `control-panel` Chapter 6 [control panel], page 58.

After you have named your machine, the next screen you are presented with is

```
+------------------------- Install Options -------------------------+
| You can use the up/down arrow keys to navigate                     |
| through the list. Press SPACE to toggle option                     |
| on or off.                                                         |
|                                                                    |
| Please see the Plug and Play manual for more information           |
| setting hard disk geometry specifications and when you             |
| should use one.                                                    |
|                                                                    |
| Select the options you desire:                                     |
| +--------------------------------------------------------------+ |
| |            [X] Automount your CD-ROM drive                    | |
| |            [X] Activate Guest Account                         | |
| |            [X] Append boot time options                       | |
| |            [X] Install LILO on master boot record             | |
| |            [X] Reboot after installation                      | |
| |            [ ] Make Boot floppy                               | |
| +--------------------------------------------------------------+ |
|                                                                    |
+--------------------------------------------------------------------+
|                      <  OK  >      <Cancel>                        |
+--------------------------------------------------------------------+
```

This screen is simply six yes or no questions that you are being asked all at once. For most users the defaults are fine; however there are circumstances when you may need to change one or more of them. An "[X]" in front of the line is equivalent to saying yes and a "[ ]" is equivalent to no. To change one of the answers, use the arrow keys to move the cursor, and press the space bar when it is over the selection you wish to change. When you are done press **ENTER** to continue, or use the right and left arrow keys to highlight cancel and press **ENTER** to exit the install script. An explanation of each of the questions follows.

Automount Your CD-ROM Drive

On boot, Plug and Play Linux has the ability to run from the CD drive any packages that have not yet been installed on the hard disk. For this feature to work, the Plug and Play Linux CD-ROM must be mounted on '/system_cd'. If you select this option (the default), then every time your system boots, it will attempt to mount the Plug and Play CD on '/system_cd'. If you do not select this option, then packages which are not installed on your hard drive will not function unless you mount the Plug and Play Linux CD manually after booting. See Section 14.4 [fstab], page 96, for information on how this is done automatically.

Activate Guest Account

The guest account is normally installed with no password and standard user privileges. This is fine on a system which is not connected to a network, or if security is not a big concern. If you do not wish the guest account to be active, then do not select this option.

Append Boot Time Options

Normally when you install Plug and Play Linux, the install script looks at what you typed at the "boot:" prompt and includes that information in '`/etc/lilo.conf`' so that when you boot from the hard drive, it is as though you typed those same options at the "boot:" prompt. If you do not want the "boot:" line you used this time to become the default, do not select this option.

Install LILO On Master Boot Record

LILO is the Linux loader; it will be installed on your hard drive. It allows you select which operating system you wish to boot, and even allows booting DOS from the second hard drive. If you already have a program which lets you select which partition to boot from, then you may not wish to install LILO on the master boot record. If you do install LILO on the master boot record, be sure to see the section of the LILO manual (in /usr/doc) on de-installing LILO before you erase anything. No matter what you select here, LILO will be put on the boot record of your root partition, so you will be able to boot Linux by making the root partition your active partition.

Reboot After Installation.

Usually the first thing you will want to do after the installation is to reboot your system and try out your new version of Linux. This option causes install to finish by prompting you to remove the boot floppy and then it attempts to reboot your system. Linux is unable to reboot some PC hardware; if your system seems to hang for more than a moment while displaying "Please wait while the system reboots" or a similar message, you probably have one of these PCs. If this happens, you will have to manually reboot the system.

Make Boot Floppy

If you do not wish to have Linux boot from your hard drive, or if you wish to have another way to boot your system, the install script will create a boot floppy which will be somewhat customized for your system. This boot floppy can also be used as an emergency recovery floppy.

2.2 Hard Disk Geometry

This section is for situations where Linux must be given the hard drive geometry explicitly. This should only occur with a few SCSI controller/hard drive combinations, or when some BIOS limitation does not allow use of all of the hard drive. Most people can safely skip this section. If you did not select "Enter Hard Disk Geometry", you will not be given an opportunity to enter the hard disk geometry, so this section is unnecessary.

If you do find it necessary to enter a hard disk geometry, you must first determine what the BIOS thinks the geometry is. Often this information is displayed at boot time, or is on one of the CMOS configuration screens. If you cannot find out what the BIOS thinks your hard drive geometry is, the SCSI howto (in '`/usr/doc`' on the CD) contains detailed instructions on how to get the geometry from DOS. If you enter the geometry incorrectly, it is possible that your partition table will corrupted leading to erratic behavior on all operating systems using that hard drive.

The screen you will see when it is time to enter the drive geometry is

```
Yggdrasil Computing, Inc.
------------------------------------------------------------------------------
-

      +---------------------- Hard Drive Geometry -----------------------+
      |                                                                  |
      |  Enter the hard drive geometry specification in the              |
      |  following format: device head sector cylinders                  |
      |                                                                  |
      |  For example, entering /dev/sda 64 32 1717 would mean that the   |
      |  first scsi hard drive (/dev/sda) has 64 heads, 32 sectors,      |
      |  and 1717 cylinders.                                             |
      |                                                                  |
      |  Please see the Plug and Play manual for more information        |
      |  on geometry specifications and when you should use one.         |
      |                                                                  |
      | +--------------------------------------------------------------+ |
      | |                                                              | |
      | +--------------------------------------------------------------+ |
      |                                                                  |
      +------------------------------------------------------------------+
      |                     <  OK  >      <Cancel>                       |
      +------------------------------------------------------------------+
```

On this screen, you may enter the geometry for any number of hard drives. The format of the geometry string is

```
<device special file> heads sectors cylinders
```

The device special file is the name of the file in '`/dev`' used to access the entire drive Chapter 13 [devices], page 88. You will most likely use one of

- '/dev/hda'
  The first IDE, RLL, MFM, or ESDI device on the first controller.
- '/dev/hdb'
  The second IDE, RLL, MFM, or ESDI device on the first controller.
- '/dev/hdc'
  The first IDE, RLL, MFM, or ESDI device on the second controller.
- '/dev/hdd'
  The second IDE, RLL, MFM, or ESDI device on the second controller.
- '/dev/sda'
  The fist SCSI hard disk detected.
- '/dev/sdb'
  The second SCSI hard disk detected.
- '/dev/sdc'
  The third SCSI hard disk detected.
- '/dev/sdd'
  The fourth SCSI hard disk detected.

For heads, sectors, and cylinders enter the values the BIOS thinks the drive has. If you need to specify the geometry for more than one drive, just put in a space and append the specification for the next drive. Continue until you have specified the geometries of all the drives you need.

Users of SCSI devices are probably wondering why all this is necessary, since at no point does Linux need to know any of this information to access a SCSI hard drive. The answer is simple; the partition table contains this information, and DOS and the BIOS use it. If the information in the partition table does not agree with what DOS and the BIOS think it is, the hard drive may not function correctly under DOS.

2.3 Checking for Linux Partitions

The next thing the install script does, is check to see if you already have Linux installed on your computer. If so, it looks for a few configuration files (most notably '/etc/fstab') and saves them for later use. If you do have Linux already installed, be sure to allow `fsck` to run `mkfs` on your root partition so that no old files are left around to cause confusion later.

```
+------------ Linux Partition Check -------------+
|                                                |
| Checking for linux partitions...               |
|                                                |
|                                                |
|                                                |
|  +-----------------------------------------+   |
|  |                  50%                    |   |
|  +-----------------------------------------+   |
+------------------------------------------------+
```

Once the install script has determined whether you already have Linux installed, the next screen you see is a message describing the types of partitions you should make.

```
+---------------------- Message from Yggdrasil ----------------------+
|                                                                    |
| This script installs a ten megabyte Plug-and-Play                  |
| Linux configuration on your hard disk, installing                  |
| everything except "/usr".  This involves partitioning              |
| your hard disk, and designating partitions for the                 |
| root filesystem, and, optionally, swap and /home                   |
| (personal directories).                                            |
|                                                                    |
| Be sure to allocate space for any optional software                |
| components that you may want to install later.  See                |
| the manual for the sizes and descriptions of optional              |
| software components.                                               |
|                                                                    |
| If you create a /home partition it will be easier for              |
| you to install subsequent CDROM distributions, since you           |
| will be able to erase your old root partition without              |
| effecting your /home partition.  Remember to leave some            |
| free space for /tmp and, if you are not creating                   |
| separate /home partition, to leave space for your home             |
| directory.                                                         |
|                                                                    |
+--------------------------------------------------------------------+
|                              < OK >                                |
+--------------------------------------------------------------------+
```

This message displayed here is not quite accurate. Before the install script exits, you will be given an opportunity to install more than just the runtime package.

This message gives you an idea of the types of partitions you may wish to make for Plug and Play Linux. Partitioning your hard drive is necessary to allow more than one operating system to share the disk space. Plug and Play Linux will allow you to install Linux on a DOS partition by using the UMSDOS file system. However, we do not recommend this because the UMSDOS file system has proven unreliable in the past, and you will not be able to boot from your hard drive (there is a program called `loadlin`, which should be on one or more of the Linux Internet Archive CDs that came as part of Plug and Play Linux, which will allow you to start Linux without a boot floppy). Please Section 2.4 [fdisk], page 17, for more information about partitioning.

There is a program, called `FIPS` in the root directory of your Plug and Play Linux CD which purports to allow you to repartition your hard disk without losing any data. This program is experimental and untested; use it at your own risk. In any event *make sure you have a recent backup before proceeding.*

If the install script detects that you already have Linux installed in its own partition, then you will see the following message:

```
+--------------------- Message from Yggdrasil ---------------------+
|                                                                  |
| Since your system already has a version of Linux                 |
| on it, you probably do not need to repartition it,               |
| however you should still check the partitioning and              |
| mount points to make sure they are the way you want              |
| them.                                                            |
|                                                                  |
| You should also have mkfs run on your root partition             |
| so that no old configuration files will be left around           |
| to cause confusion.                                              |
|                                                                  |
+------------------------------------------------------------------+
|                            <  OK  >                              |
+------------------------------------------------------------------+
```

This message is just reiterating what was said before. Since you already have partitioned your hard drive for Linux, you do not need to repartition it. However, you should still run `mkfs` on your root partition to delete any old files.

If the install script does not find Linux already on a partition of its own, then you should see the following message:

```
+----------------- Message from Yggdrasil -----------------+
|                                                           |
| Since Linux is not currently installed on your            |
| system, be sure to allow the installation procedure       |
| to run mkfs or mkswap on your partitions.                 |
|                                                           |
|                                                           |
+-----------------------------------------------------------+
|                         <  OK  >                          |
+-----------------------------------------------------------+
```

This message is telling you that since Linux was not already found on your system, the partitions you create for it will need to be formatted. You will be asked if you want the partitions formatted.

2.4 fdisk

fdisk is a menu driven program for manipulation of the hard disk partition table. The device is usually one of the following:

/dev/hda /dev/hdb /dev/sda /dev/sdb The partition is a device name followed by a partition number. For example, /dev/hda1 is the first partition on the first hard disk in the system.

If possible, fdisk will obtain the disk geometry automati- cally. This is not necessarily the physical disk geome- try, but is the disk geometry that MS-DOS uses for the partition table. If fdisk warns you that you need to set the disk geometry, please believe this statement, and set the geometry. This should only be necessary with certain SCSI host adapters (the drivers for which are rapidly being modified to provide geometry information automatically).

To discover the many commands available for fdisk, use the m (menu) command. This will display a list of commands available. The commonly used commands are:

p - print out the partition table. d - delete a partition. n - add a partition. w - write out the partition table.

After creating a new partition table, it is possible that you need to reboot your computer before the new partition table takes effect. This should only happen if you were experimenting with your system and left the hard drive mounted. If this happens, you will see the following message:

```
+--------------------- Message from Yggdrasil ---------------------+
| You must now reboot your computer so Linux can                    |
| reread the partition tables.                                      |
|                                                                   |
| To continue the installation, login as 'install'                  |
| again, and exit the fstab editor after setting                    |
| up the mount points.                                              |
|                                                                   |
|                                                                   |
+-------------------------------------------------------------------+
|                              <  OK  >                             |
+-------------------------------------------------------------------+
```

If this happens, some of the '`/etc/fstab`' information may be lost; you may need to change the mountpoints for some of the partitions when you re-run install.

2.5 Configuration

The last question that is asked before the actual installation begins, is exactly how much material you wish to install at this time.

```
Yggdrasil Computing, Inc.
------------------------------------------------------------------------------
-
           +------------------- Configuration -------------------+
           |                                                     |
           |                                                     |
           |  You can use the up/down arrow keys to navigate     |
           |  through the list. Press SPACE to toggle option     |
           |  on or off.                                         |
           |                                                     |
           |  Which configuration would you like installed on    |
           |  your hard disk?:                                   |
           |                                                     |
           | +-------------------------------------------------+ |
           | |         ( ) Runtime                 10 MB       | |
           | |         (*) Strongly Recommended    30 MB       | |
           | |         ( ) Suggested               250 MB      | |
           | |         ( ) Everything              600 MB      | |
           | +-------------------------------------------------+ |
           |                                                     |
           +-----------------------------------------------------+
           |               <  OK  >      <Cancel>                |
           +-----------------------------------------------------+
```

You select how much of Plug and Play Linux you wish installed on your hard drive. Remember that so long as the Plug and Play Linux CD is mounted on '/system_cd' you will still be able to run everything. Software not on your hard drive will simply be slow. You can also easily install individual packages later from the control panel. The sizes given are only estimates, and are not meant to be precise.

2.6 The Copying Begins

The following message will appear on your screen for a short while as the install script mounts your hard drive.

```
+--- Message from Yggdrasil -----+
|                                |
|   Mounting Partitions          |
|                                |
+--------------------------------+
```

After a few seconds, this message will disappear and be replaced by

```
+---- Message from Yggdrasil -----+
| The runtime system will now be  |
| installed on your harddrive.    |
+---------------------------------+
|             <  OK  >            |
+---------------------------------+
```

The real purpose of this message is to give those people who already have Linux installed one last chance to quit before their entire system is overwritten. Press ENTER when you are ready to continue.

At this point the runtime system will be copied from your CD to your hard drive. While this is occurring, the following message will be displayed.

```
+------------- Message from Yggdrasil --------------+
|                                                    |
| The installation script will now begin copying    |
| the files from the CDROM to your hard disk.       |
| This may take enough time for the screen saver    |
| to activate.  To wake up the screen saver without |
| sending additional characters to the installation |
| script, hit a key on the keyboard that does not   |
| send characters by itself, like one of the shift  |
| keys, for example.                                 |
|                                                    |
|  +------------------------------------------+     |
|  |                  50%                     |     |
|  +------------------------------------------+     |
+----------------------------------------------------+
```

After copying the runtime package to your hard drive, the install script then generates '/etc/fstab' (See Section 14.4 [fstab], page 96.) While this is happening, you will see the message

```
Yggdrasil Computing, Inc.
-----------------------------------------------------------------------------
-


              +----------- Message from Yggdrasil -----------+
              |                                              |
              | Generating /etc/fstab...                     |
              |                                              |
              |  +---------------------------------------+  |
              |  |                 50%                   |  |
              |  +---------------------------------------+  |
              +----------------------------------------------+
```

After a few seconds, you will see the message

```
Yggdrasil Computing, Inc.
--------------------------------------------------------------------------------
-


                    +------- Message from Yggdrasil -------+
                    |                                      |
                    | Configuring kernel...                |
                    |                                      |
                    |  +--------------------------------+  |
                    |  |              50%               |  |
                    |  +--------------------------------+  |
                    +--------------------------------------+
```

At this point, the install script is creating '/etc/lilo.conf' and changing the kernel configuration. Even if you do not use LILO, '/etc/lilo.conf' is necessary to create boot floppies.

If you asked for a boot floppy to be made, then you will see the following

```
     +------------------------- Make Boot Floppy -------------------------+
     |                                                                    |
     | Insert a blank diskette into drive A and hit RETURN.               |
     |                                                                    |
     |                                                                    |
     +--------------------------------------------------------------------+
     |                             <  OK  >                               |
     +--------------------------------------------------------------------+
```

Insert a blank high density diskette into your first floppy drive and press return. In a few moments a boot floppy will be created.

Now, if you asked for more than the runtime package to be installed, you will see the following message

```
              +------------ Message from Yggdrasil ------------+
              | Installing ...                                 |
              |     (This may take a while)                    |
              |                                                |
              +------------------------------------------------+
```

Depending on how much you asked to have installed and the speed of your CD-ROM drive, this could take an hour or more. When it is finally finished, if you asked for the system to be rebooted, you will see

```
+------- Message from Yggdrasil -------+
| Please remove the boot floppy        |
| so that the system can reboot...     |
+--------------------------------------+
|                < OK >                |
+--------------------------------------+
```

If you did not ask for the system to be rebooted, then you will see

```
+--------------------- Message from Yggdrasil ----------------------+
|                                                                   |
| That completes the installation.  Now would be a good             |
| time to try booting your newly installed system.                  |
|                                                                   |
| If you want to try booting your system from the hard              |
| disk, shut down the system (log in as root, issue the             |
| "halt" command, and wait for the message that it's okay           |
| to turn the power off), remove the floppy disk                    |
| if there is one in the drive and reset the computer.              |
|                                                                   |
| When you start X windows with the "xinit" command                 |
| for the first time, you will automatically be prompted            |
| for X configuration information.  Once you have started           |
| X windows, you can make some other system configuration           |
| changes by running the "control-panel" program as                 |
| root.  (Do a "control-panel &" from a root shell in an            |
| xterm window.)                                                    |
|                                                                   |
+-------------------------------------------------------------------+
|                             < OK >                                |
+-------------------------------------------------------------------+
```

or if you asked the system to reboot automatically, you will see

```
+------- Message from Yggdrasil -------+
| Please remove the boot floppy        |
| so that the system can reboot...     |
+--------------------------------------+
|                < OK >                |
+--------------------------------------+
```

At this point the installation is finished. After you reboot, Linux will be running from your hard drive.

2.7 Installing when Linux Cannot Find Your CD-ROM Drive

As mentioned before, Plug and Play Linux has several installation methods, some of which are useful when your hardware is not fully supported. So long as Linux can find your hard drive, you should be able to install and run Plug and Play Linux.

2.7.1 Installing with NFS

If Linux cannot find your CD-ROM drive, or if you wish to install Linux on many machines over a network, then the NFS install is probably the best choice. It is essentially the same as a normal install except that instead of using a local CD-ROM for Linux, you install from another computer on your network that has disc 1 of Plug and Play Linux (or a copy of it) mounted and exported by NFS. The NFS server does not have to be running Linux, but it must have the CDROM mounted and it must support the Rockridge ISO-9660 CDROM extensions (most unix-like systems do).

The first step in doing a network install is to create a network install boot floppy on a 1.44M floppy disk. One of the options of creating a Linux boot floppy is creating a network boot floppy.

Next, boot from the boot floppy as if you are doing a normal install. At the "boot:" prompt type

```
boot: linux ramdisk=1440 root=/dev/fd0
```

This will load the contents of the floppy into the ramdisk, and mount it as root.

You will be asked several questions about your network and NFS server. After answering these questions, you will be connected to your NFS server, and the installation will proceed as before.

2.7.2 Installing from within DOS to a UMSDOS File System

This version of Plug and Play Linux lets you install under DOS from an unsupported CD-ROM or even over a DOS network. This installation procedure is still experimental and it will be necessary to do some configuration manually after you have booted into Linux. This installation does not require you to re-partition your DOS drive.

To do a DOS install, you must cd to the Yggdrasil Plug and Play CD-ROM and then cd to the \dosbin directory. While in that directory, you type

lbase src: dest:

where src: is the CD-ROM drive letter and dest: is the hard drive letter where you are installing Linux (e.g. lbase g: c:).

After the UMSDOS file system is made, you can install any desired software packages by typing linstall packagename src: dest: from the Plug and Play \dosbin directory (e.g. linstall usrbin g: c:).

After Linux is installed in this manner, you can invoke it by running the batch file linux.bat located in the directory where Linux was installed. In other words, just type linux and you'll be up and running! If you get the message "Not enough memory below 90000h" remove some of your loaded drivers or TSR programs, or use a memory manager program such as `EMM386.EXE` to load DOS and your drivers/TSRs high.

3 Forcing Hardware Detection

Since Linux runs in 32 bit protected mode, it cannot use any 16 bit device drivers or BIOS code; hence most drivers supplied by hardware vendors will not work. Furthermore, some hardware is unsuitable for use in a multi-user, multi-tasking environment such as Linux. That said, most common PC hardware is supported by Linux.

3.1 The "boot:" Prompt.

If your hardware is not automatically detected by Linux, it is possible that the kernel is looking in the wrong place. Often vendors and OEMs will change I/O ports on hardware that is otherwise identical to supported hardware. If this is the case, then often all you need to do is type in an appropriate command at the "boot:" prompt.

Every command you type at the "boot:" prompt must begin with the name of the kernel you wish to boot followed by a space. Normally this is "linux". The rest of the line consists of a list of commands, separated by a space, that control kernel initialization or are passed on to `init`. As of kernel version 1.2.9, the following kernel commands are understood:

reserve=i/o range
: Reserves a range of I/O ports. No drivers should look at any of these addresses, but some older ones still do.

ramdisk=size in K
: Reserves memory for a ramdisk. Future kernel versions will have a ramdisk which can be configured at runtime instead of at boot time.

ether=irq,io port,memory start,memor_end,interface
: Specifies the location of a network card. Use -1 for parameters which do not apply to your ethernet card. Interface is normally one of `eth0` or `eth1`.

max_scsi_luns=7
: If you have a SCSI adapter and a SCSI device which uses a LUN greater than 1, such as some CD-Changers, you will need to add this line to your boot prompt.

hda=

hdb=

hdc=

hdd=

hd= Used to control (E)IDE devices. Use one of `dtc2278`, `serialize`, `noprobe`, `cdrom`, or cylinders,heads,sectors,write-precomp,irq. Under most circumstances you should never need to use any of these commands; however, if you have a buggy EIDE controller, then you may need to use one of `dtc2278`, `serialize`, or `noprobe`. If your CMOS incorrectly reports the geometry of your hard drive, you may need to tell Linux about the cylinders, heads, and sectors explicitly. The write-precomp and irq are optional in most circumstances. Finally if you have an ATAPI CD-ROM drive which is not detected you can tell Linux about it explicitly. For example if you have a CD-ROM as the master device on a secondary EIDE controller, you may need to use the line '`linux hdc=cdrom`' if Linux is unable to detect it on its own.

st=buffer_size,write_threshold
This lets you adjust the buffer size and write threshold for SCSI tapes to improve efficiency. You should not need to change this to install Plug and Play Linux.

busmouse=irq
This sets the interrupt for a Logitech Bus Mouse.

st0x=memory,irq
Use this if you have a Seagate ST-01 or ST-02 which is not automatically detected. For example

```
boot: linux st0x=0xc8000,5
```

if you have a Seagate ST-01 or ST-02 controller on irq 5 at memory address C800h. The extra 0 is necessary because the address you pass to Linux is a linear address while DOS and the BIOS use segmented addresses. If your memory address already has 5 or more hex digits, then do not append an extra 0.

tmc8xx=memory,irq
Use this if you have a Future Domain TMC-800 series or TMC-950 SCSI controller which is not automatically detected.

t128=memory,irq
Use this if you have a Trantor T128,T128F, or T288 adapter which is not automatically detected.

pas16=io_port,irq
Use this if you have a ProAudio Spectrum 16 SCSI controller which is not automatically detected. If you are not using an interrupt use `pas16=io_port,255`. For the default configuration, use `pas16=0x388,255`.

ncr5380=port,irq,dma
: Use this if you have a generic SCSI adapter based on the ncr5380 chipset which is not detected. The Trantor T130 is such a controller.

aha152x=port,irq,scsi-id,reconnect,parity
: Use this to force detection of an Adaptec 1510, 1520, or other SCSI adapter based on the Adaptec AIC-6260 chip. For normal use, SCSI-id should be 7, reconnect should be 0 or 1, and parity should also be 0 or 1.

aha1542=io_port,buson,busoff,dmaspeed
: Under normal circumstances, use of this command line parameter is unnecessary. However if you wish to experiment read the file '`/usr/src/linux/drivers/scsi/aha1542.c`' for information on what the parameters mean.

aic7xxx=extended,no_reset
: Again, these should not be necessary under normal use. For your information, extended turns on extended translation, and no_reset causes the driver to never reset the SCSI bus.

buslogic=io_port
: Use this if you have a buslogic SCSI controller which is not automatically detected.

xd=type,irq,io,dma
: If you have an old xt-style hard drive controller, you may need to specify this line. See '`/usr/src/linux/drivers/block/xd.c`' for more info.

floppy=number,parameter
: If you have problems with your floppy drive, you can adjust several parameters with this command. The supported parameters are

  - allowed_drive_mask
  - all_drives
  - asus_pci
  - daring
  - two_fdc
  - one_fdc
  - thinkpad
  - cmos
  - unexpected_interrupts
  - no_unexpected_interrupts

- L40SX

mcd=io_port,irq,workaround
Use this command if you have an older (non-ATAPI, non-IDE) Mitsumi CD-ROM drive which is not being detected. There are some problems with a few very old Mitsumi CD-ROM drives. Setting workaround to 1 will cause Linux to access the CD-ROM more slowly than normal, to prevent these problems from affecting operation.

aztcd=io_port.controller
Use this if you have an older (non-ATAPI, non-IDE) Wearnes, Orchid, or Aztech CD-Rom drive which is not detected.

sonycd535=io_port
Use this if you have a Sony 535 CD-ROM drive which is not detected.

sound=flags
This will force detection of your sound card. For more information, see /usr/src/linux/drivers/sound/dev_table.c.

sbpcd=io_port,type
If you have a CD-ROM drive connected to a proprietary 100\% Sound Blaster compatible interface, then use this option to force detection. Type is one of SoundBlaster, LaserMate, or SPEA and io_port must be the io_port of the CD-ROM controller, not the sound portion of the card. Use `sbpcd=0` to skip the lengthy probe for Sound Blaster CD-ROMs.

cdu31a=io_port,irq,type
Probing for Sony CDU 31As and CDU33's has been disabled since the probe routines caused problems. If you have one of these drives that you wish to use under Linux, you must provide the io_port and irq explicitly, or you can activate the probe routines by typing `cdu31a=probe`. Currently type should be left blank unless you have a ProAudio Spectrum style interface in which case it should be PAS.

mscdex=0 This parameter will allow Linux to use a DOS MSCDEX driver to access a CD-ROM drive. Linux must have been loaded specially (using dosload) and the CD-ROM driver must be well behaved. The use of this option is not recommended.

bios_hd=0 If you set this parameter to 1, then Linux will attempt to access your hard drive via the BIOS. This does *not* shut off any other attempts to access your hard drive. Use only if you have a completely unsupported hard drive and then use with caution.

no_bios=0 This parameter must be set to 1 for the MSCDEX driver of the BIOS hard drive to work. Use of either of these drivers is strongly discouraged.

ncr53c810=mem,io,irq
ncr53c810=,bus,device,function,pci
Since the ncr53c810 is a PCI controller, you should never need to use this option, but you want to, please take a look at /usr/src/linux/drivers/scsi/53c7,8xx.c.

fd16x0=bios,flags,major,minor
fdomain=bios,flags,major,minor
These two commands are equivalent. Use them if you have a Future Domain 16x0 series which is not automatically detected. This happens because Future Domain's controller BIOS signatures are inconsistent.

eata=port Use this if you have an EATA compatible SCSI adapter which is not automatically detected.

in2000=io_port
Use this if you have an in2000 card which is not detected.

iomega=io_port
Use this if you have an iomega_pc2 adapter which is not detected.

qlogic=io_port
Use this if you have a QLOGIC SCSI adapter which is not detected.

ultrastor1434=io_port
Use this if you have an Ultrastore 14f or 34f which is not detected and you are using the driver which supports only the 14f and 34f.

ultrastor24f=io_port
Use this if you have an Ultrastore 14f, 24f, or 34f which is not detected and you are using the driver which supports all three.

wd7000=bios_addr,io_port,irq,dma
Use this if you have a Western Digital Fast SCSI controller which is not being detected.

4 Booting

In this chapter we will briefly discuss the two methods that Plug and Play Linux can use for booting. Unlike DOS, which can use the BIOS to access hardware at boot time, Linux must have special drivers for every piece of hardware it wishes to access, and also must be able to locate that hardware on the bus. For relatively standard hardware, such as IDE hard drives, this is not a problem. For other hardware, such as certain SCSI controllers, it is not possible to do without crashing the system. To get around this problem, both LILO and SYSLINUX provide methods for the user to specify hardware configuration parameters.

4.1 LILO

LILO allows for the specification of some configuration parameters at the 'boot:' prompt. The format of the command line is the image to boot followed by a space followed by the parameters to be passed to the kernel. A complete list of parameters the kernel understands is given in the section on Hardware Configuration. An example command line is

```
linux aha152x=0x300,5,7,1 ro
```

to load the image named linux and tell it you have an Adaptec 1520 controller at I/O port 0x300, IRQ 5, with SCSI id 7 and that it should do asynchronous I/O. The 'ro' tells the system to mount the root partition read-only.

4.1.1 Booting with LILO

As the system is booting, you will be presented with a boot prompt. This will enable you to select the desired boot configuration. You can discover what is available by pressing the TAB key. Each item available represents a stanza in the /etc/lilo.conf file. This could be another Linux kernel, DOS, or anything else that you configure in that file.

4.1.2 LILO Configuration

With the command line method of configuring LILO, the user must type in configuration information every time the system is booted. By using a configuration file, LILO can be configured once and then the system will boot unattended. A summary of the LILO configuration file is provided here. For more complete information on the options available with LILO, see the LILO documentation in '`/usr/doc`'.

The LILO configuration file is kept in '/etc/lilo.conf' and consists of a series of variable assignments and comments. An example LILO configuration file is

```
timeout=100
prompt
install = /boot/boot.b
boot=/dev/sda
#compact # accelerates booting, but breaks on Diamond motherboards
linear # will still work even if the bios geometry and linux
# geometry don't match
#delay = 0 # optional, for systems that boot very quickly
vga = normal # force sane state
ramdisk = 0 # paranoia setting
root = # use "current" root
map = /boot/map
read-only
message = /boot/boot.message
append = "aha152x=0x300,5,7,1"
image = /vmlinux
label = linux
image = /zImage
label = test
root = /dev/sda2
optional
```

Comments begin with a '#' and continue until the end of the line, so lines like

```
#delay = 0 # optional, for systems that boot very quickly
```

are commented out while lines like

```
vga = normal # force sane state
```

are in effect for the first half of the line, up to the '#'; the rest of the line is ignored.

Each non-blank, non-comment line has some effect on the boot process. The most common one to change is the `append` line.

The `append` line tells LILO to append the given string to the arguments passed by the kernel. This is effectively the same as typing the string on the command line *every time the system is booted*. This is the preferred method of telling Linux about hardware it can't find out about on it's own.

In the above example, the `append` line appears before any of the `image` lines, so it will affect all the images. If the `append` line appeared after an `image` line, it would only affect the image of which it was part. In this way it is possible to have different images with different command lines passed to the kernel. This is not as useful with the `append` command as it is with the other commands that work similarly, such as `ramdisk`, `read_only`, `read-write`, `root`, and `vga`.

Adding other boot images is as simple as adding new `image` or `other` sections. An `image` section is used to boot Linux, and a `other` section is used to boot all other operating systems. An `image` section consists of the line

```
image = <file>
```

where '`<file>`' is the full path to the Linux kernel you wish to boot, followed by the line

```
label = <name>
```

where `<name>` is the name you wish to call the image. Then typing the image name at the `boot:` prompt will boot the selected kernel. You can then follow the `label` line with image specific parameters such as `root`, `read-only`, or `append`.

4.1.3 Running LILO

In order for any changes made to '`lilo.conf`' to take effect, or if a kernel image has been updated, '`/sbin/lilo`' must be run *before rebooting*. To run LILO, log in as `root` and type `lilo`. You should see something similar to

```
# lilo
Added linux *
Added test
```

What you see will of course differ depending on what you have in '`lilo.conf`'. When you have first installed Plug and Play Linux, the install scripts create boot entries for each of the partitions which might possibly be bootable, so you will see entries similar to `hda1`, `hda2`,

... for IDE base systems, or `sda1`, `sda2`,

... or SCSI based systems.

4.2 I

Using LILO for floppies can be difficult. Furthermore, those floppies can only be modified under Linux creating something of a chicken and egg problem. H. Peter Avin solved this problem by creating SYSLINUX. SYSLINUX works by replacing the standard DOS boot information on a DOS floppy with something that will load Linux instead of DOS. The big advantage of this method is that all the files are DOS files and can be changed *before* Linux is running. To upgrade a kernel under SYSLINUX one need only use the DOS copy command. The boot floppies that come with Plug and Play Linux use SYSLINUX for this reason.

4.2.1 Boot Parameters

With the exception of the TAB key not listing the choice of images and the vga option not working, the boot: prompt is the same as with LILO. See See Section 4.1 [LILO], page 30.

Multiple Linux kernels can be stored under different names and configured in the /etc/lilo.conf file. This is particularly useful when you are customizing your kernel and you want to be assured of being able to get back to your old kernel in case something goes wrong.

You may also use the boot floppy in case something goes wrong with LILO. Simply supply the location of the root partition at the boot prompt. For example,

```
boot: linux root=/dev/hdb1
```

4.2.2 Updating the kernel

The original purpose of SYSLINUX was to make upgrading the kernel on the boot floppy easy. To upgrade the boot floppy, one just copies the kernel image onto the floppy. To copy a kernel called 'linux' in the current directory onto the boot floppy under DOS you insert the floppy into drive a: and type

```
copy linux a:
```

Under Linux you must first mount the floppy, and then copy the file over. This is accomplished by typing

```
mount -t msdos /dev/fd0 /mnt
cp linux /mnt
umount /mnt
```

See Section 4.2.1 [Booting with SYSLINUX], page 33.

4.2.3 Configuring SYSLINUX

SYSLINUX is configured in much the same way as LILO. See Section 4.1.2 [LILO config], page 30 The file to edit is 'syslinux.cfg' in the root directory of the floppy. This file can be edited under either DOS or Linux. Under Linux use an editor such as vi Section 16.5.3 [vi], page 107, or emacs Section 16.5.1 [emacs], page 106. Under DOS use a *text editor* such as edit; do *not* use a word processor. If it is absolutely necessary to use a word processor, be sure to save the file as ascii/text; any other format will cause unpredictable results. The format of this file is similar to that of LILO. See Section 4.1.2

[LILO config], page 30. Lines beginning with '#' and Blank lines are ignored. The keywords that SYSLINUX understands are

- `default` *kernel options* Sets the default command line as though you had type it at the `boot:` prompt.
- `append` *options* Adds options to the `boot:` line for all boots. This is similar to the LILO append command.
- `timeout` *value* Indicates how long to wait at the `boot:` prompt until booting automatically with the Default command line.
- `display` *filename* Prints the contents of '`filename`' on the screen at boot time before the `boot:` prompt. This file should be a DOS text file with CR+LF and the end of each line.
- `prompt` *flag* If the flag is 0, display the `boot:` prompt only if the Shift or Alt key is pressed, or Caps Lock or Scroll lock is set. If flag is 1, the `boot:` prompt is always displayed.

The only time a user should need to change this file is when using a floppy to boot, and you wish to add kernel options to the command line.

5 Recompiling the Kernel

The Linux kernel is the program which talks to the hardware, schedules tasks, keeps one program from crashing another, and basically allows all the other other programs to work without conflict. The kernel which comes with Plug and Play Linux supports the widest variety of hardware possible within the size limitations enforced by using the 16 bit BIOS at load time. This means that you may have hardware which is supported by Linux, but not by the default kernel, or more likely, there is hardware supported by the default kernel which you do not have. In the latter case, the drivers are taking up memory, and perhaps even confusing hardware which you do have. In either case you should recompile the kernel so it supports as much of your hardware as possible and little else.

Before you can recompile the kernel, you must first make sure the source is on the hard drive, and not the CD-ROM. See the installation instructions to see how to do this, or type `install_path /system_cd/usr/src/linux` if the Plug and Play CD is mounted on '`/system_cd`'. If you are logged in as root and get `Permission denied` or `Readonly Filesystem` errors, you probably have not installed the kernel source onto your hard drive.

5.1 Configuring the Kernel

The first step in recompiling the kernel is to configure it. To do this type:

```
cd /usr/src/linux
make config
```

You will then be asked a number of questions about what you want included in the kernel. As of Linux version 1.2.8, you will be asked the following questions, some of which will be skipped depending on your answers to earlier questions.

Kernel math emulation

Linux software assumes that you have a math co-processor. If you do not, the kernel is able to emulate one, although at a great loss of speed. If you do have a math co-processor, and still compile in the option, all you will lose is some memory; the math co-processor will still be detected and used. If you plan on using this kernel on a machine which does not have a math co-processor (386's without 387's, 486 SX's and some clones) you should answer yes to this question.

Kill Memory Hogs

This activates experimental code developed at Yggdrasil which will send a signal to the single largest running process when swap space runs out. Under most circumstances you do not need this;

however if you are working with buggy programs which tend to use too much memory and apparently hang the system, this may help. (In this case the system is not really hung, but just trying too hard to run the bad process. Eventually it will give up and processes will start dying off. However this often takes a long time.)

Normal floppy disk support
: This will allow you to access your floppy drive under Linux. You probably should answer 'y' to this.

Normal (MFM/RLL) disk and IDE disk/cdrom support
: This allows you to access most (E)IDE, MFM, RLL, and ESDI drives as well as ATAPI compliant EIDE CD-ROMs. If you have a SCSI system, you may wish to answer 'n' to this. Otherwise you should answer 'y'.

Use old disk-only driver for primary i/f
: In general you should answer 'n' to this question. If you have an older IDE, MFM, RLL, or ESDI drive which is not supported by the newer driver, you can try answering 'y' here, but it will probably not work any better.

Use new IDE driver for primary/secondary i/f
: If you see this question you should answer 'y'.

Include new IDE driver for secondary i/f support
: If you see this question, it means that you are using the old driver for your hard disk. You need to answer 'y' to this question if you have an (E)IDE controller at the secondary address which you wish to be able to access under Linux. Otherwise you should answer 'n'.

XT hard disk support
: You need to answer 'y' to this question if you have an old PC-XT style hard drive controller installed and wish to access it under Linux, otherwise answer 'n'.

BIOS callback support
: This activates experimental code developed at Yggdrasil, which allows Linux to access the 16 bit BIOS and, under some circumstances, DOS device drivers. Because of the poor way in which most 16 bit code has been written, the result of using this code is often a crash. However it has proven useful for many people to access otherwise unsupported CD-ROMS and hard disks. Unless you are a developer and/or know what you are doing, or are desperate to access a particular device, you should answer 'n' here.

BIOS hard disk support
: This includes experimental code to access the hard drive via BIOS calls. See the warnings above under BIOS callback support to determine under what circumstances to answer 'y' to this.

Networking support
: In general, you should answer 'y' to this question. Under some circumstances you can save memory by answering 'n' here, but any program which uses networking, including `lpr`, `syslogd`, and `X`, will not work as expected, or more likely not at all.

Limit memory to low 16MB
: In general you should answer 'n' to this question. However if you have more than 16 megabytes of memory and are using a device driver which attempts to do DMA over the ISA bus without using bounce buffers, you should answer 'y' here. All the mainstream drivers use bounce buffers when necessary, so the only time this should be required is when developing or testing a new device driver.

PCI bios support
: If you plan to use this kernel on a PCI machine, you should answer 'y' to this question, otherwise 'n'. Be warned that currently this option and the BIOS callback support are mutually incompatible.

PCI bridge optimization (experimental)
: This will activate code which attempts to optimize certain uses of the PCI bus. It is currently experimental, and you should answer 'n' to this unless you need to be on the cutting edge, or wish to test the code with your system.

System V IPC
: IPC stands for inter-process communication. If you answer 'y' to this you will activate the System V style IPC which includes things such as semaphores, message queues, and certain types of shared memory. Some programs do use this, so in general you should answer 'y'; however, if you need to save some memory and know that none of your programs use this type of communication, you may answer 'n'.

Kernel support for ELF binaries
: Linux is switching to the ELF format for executables. Since Plug and Play Linux has already made most of the transition, (In fact much of the ground work for running an ELF only system was done at Yggdrasil) you will not be able to use Linux effectively unless you answer 'y' here.

Use -mpentium flag for Pentium-specific optimizations.
As the pentium optimizer for GCC has become more stable, the `-mpentium flag` has become useful. The code produced should still work on 486's, but since as of this writing the pentium version of GCC was still not stable enough for production use, 'n' is probably the correct answer to this question.

Use -m486 flag for 486-specific optimizations
Unless the kernel will be run primarily on 386's, you should answer 'y' to this question.

Set version information on all symbols for modules
Loadable device drivers under Linux are called modules. See Section 5.4 [Kernel Modules], page 50. Currently they are kernel version specific, but by including version information for each symbol, it is possible to make them less so. You should answer 'y' to this question if you plan on using loadable modules.

TCP/IP networking
If you plan on using any of the networking features of Linux you should answer 'y' to this question.

IP forwarding/gatewaying
If you intend to put your Linux box on two different networks and have it forward packets between them, or have it act as a SLIP or PPP server, you should answer 'y' to this question. Otherwise you can save a few bytes of memory by answering 'n'.

IP multicasting
IP multicasting is a way of sending network packets to many hosts at once. Unless you know you are going to be using an application which requires multicasting, it's probably better to answer 'n' here.

IP accounting
If you wish to keep track of what sort of network packets are passing through your machine, answer 'y' here. Ip accounting can also be useful for debugging purposes. However for most users 'n' is the correct answer.

PC/TCP compatibility mode
Many TCP protocol stacks for PCs tend to lie about their window size. If you answer 'y' to this, Linux will attempt to compensate by being less efficient. As of kernel version 1.2.5 there were still bugs in the Linux networking code which can cause TCP connections to some PC TCP protocol stacks to hang when large quantities of data are transferred. There were fixes for this that were removed from the kernel long ago for some unknown reason.

Reverse ARP
: This allows Linux to help certain machines to remote boot. In general `bootp` does a better job and should be used instead. You should answer 'n' to this unless you know you need it.

Assume subnets are local
: This activates an optimization and in general you should answer 'y' here.

Disable NAGLE algorithm (normally enabled)
: In general you should answer 'n' here. Answer 'y' here only if you understand the NAGLE algorithm and have a good reason to disable it.

The IPX protocol
: This allows Linux to forward IPX packets, but not to send and receive them. If you are using your Linux box as a bridge to a Novell network, you should answer 'y' here, otherwise 'n'.

SCSI support
: If you have a supported SCSI adapter and you wish to access the devices on your SCSI bus, you should answer 'y' here, otherwise 'n'.

SCSI disk support
: If you have a SCSI disk or plan on adding one in the future, you should answer 'y' here.

SCSI tape support
: If you have a SCSI tape drive or plan on adding one in the future, you should answer 'y' here.

SCSI CD-ROM support
: If you have a SCSI CD-ROM or plan on adding one in the future, you should answer 'y' here.

SCSI generic support
: If you answer 'y' here, programs will be able to access devices on the SCSI bus directly via device special files in '`/dev`'. Certain programs such as `cdwrite` (developed at Yggdrasil) use this feature to drive devices which would otherwise be unusable under Linux.

Probe all LUNs on each SCSI device.
: Some devices such as CD jukeboxes use more than one LUN. If you wish to support such a device answer 'y' here. The downside is that certain older SCSI devices will lock up the SCSI bus if you answer 'y' here. Interestingly enough, certain SCSI jukeboxes that pretend to be multiple devices can cause Linux to hang

when multiple CDs are accessed simultaneously. Code to help alleviate this problem has been developed at Yggdrasil and is included on the Plug and Play CD-ROM.

Adaptec AHA152X support
If you have a SCSI adapter based on the Adaptec AIC-6250 chipset, you should answer 'y' to this question, otherwise 'n'. If you had to use a command at the 'boot:' prompt which began "aha152x=" then you need this driver. Many SCSI adapters on sound cards require this driver as well as the Adaptec 1510 and 1520 controllers.

Adaptec AHA1542 support
If you have an Adaptec 1542 controller or compatible, you should answer 'y' here.

Adaptec AHA1740 support
If you have an Adaptec 1740 adapter running in Enhanced mode, you should answer 'y' here.

Adaptec AHA274x/284x/294x support
If you have a SCSI adapter based on the Adaptec AIC 7000 series of chips you should answer 'y' here. Current versions of the 2940 driver require that the adapter's BIOS be active, which seems to require a hard drive connected to the SCSI adapter and that the 2940 be the first controller found by the BIOS.

BusLogic SCSI support
If you have a Buslogic SCSI controller, you should answer 'y' to here.

EATA-DMA (DPT, NEC&ATT for ISA,EISA,PCI) support.
If you have a SCSI adapter from one of these manufacturers, you should answer 'y' here.

UltraStor 14F/34F support
If you have an UltraStor 14F or 34F (but not the 24F) you should answer 'y' here.

Future Domain 16xx SCSI support
If you have one of the Future Domain 1600 series SCSI adapters, you should answer 'y' here. Since the driver locates the card by looking for the signature in ROM, and Future Domain seems to change these signatures often, your card may not work if it is newer than your kernel.

Generic NCR5380 SCSI support
If you have a SCSI adapter based on the NCR5380 chipset, answer 'y'. Examples of such controllers include the Trantor T130

as well as the SCSI controller on some sound cards. If you had to use a command at the `boot:` prompt which began "ncr5380=", then you should answer 'y' here.

NCR53c7,8xx SCSI support
If you have a PCI SCSI adapter based on the 53c810 chipset (as of this writing no others are known to work) you should answer 'y' to this question. Currently most of the SCSI adapters embedded on the motherboard are based on this chipset, as well as several inexpensive PCI cards.

Always IN2000 SCSI support (test release)
If you have an Always IN2000, you need to answer 'y' here. As mentioned above, this driver is still in the testing phase and may not be reliable on your hardware.

Alway AL500 SCSI support
If you have an Always AL500 SCSI adapter, you should answer 'y' here.

IOMEGA PC2/2B SCSI support
If you have an IOMEGA PC2/2B SCSI adapter, you should answer 'y' here. The driver has some compile time options you may wish to modify (see '`/usr/src/linux/drivers/scsi/iomega_pc2.c`').

PAS16 SCSI support
If you have a ProAudio Spectrum 16 sound card with a SCSI adapter on it, you should answer 'y' to this question.

QLOGIC SCSI support
If you have a SCSI adapter made by QLOGIC, you should answer 'y' here.

Seagate ST-02 and Future Domain TMC-8xx SCSI support
If you have a Seagate ST-01, ST-02, Future Domain TMC-885 or Future Domain TMC-950, you should answer 'y' to this question.

Trantor T128/T128F/T228 SCSI support
If you have one of the SCSI adapters mentioned above, answer 'y' here.

UltraStor SCSI support
This driver purports to work with the UltraStor 14F, 24F, and 34F. If you have the 24F or if the other UltraStor driver does not work with your 14F or 34F, answer 'y' here.

7000FAST SCSI support
If you have the Western Digital 7000FAST SCSI adapter answer 'y' here.

EATA ISA/EISA (DPT PM2011/021/012/022/122/322) support.
If you have one of the SCSI adapters listed above, you should answer 'y' here.

SCSI debugging host adapter
If you are debugging a high or mid level SCSI driver, you may wish to use this pseudo-device for testing. Otherwise answer 'n'.

Network Device Support
If you wish to have any network connections to other computers, including SLIP, PLIP or PPP, you must answer 'y' here. If the loopback device is sufficient, you may answer 'n'.

Dummy net driver support
Under Linux, it is impossible to have more IP addresses than network devices. Therefore the Dummy net driver was created to allow extra IP addresses. If you need more IP addresses than you have net connections, which is often the case if your Linux box is going to be a SLIP server or gateway, you should answer 'y' here.

SLIP (serial line) support
If you wish to use the Serial Line Internet Protocol (SLIP), you should answer 'y' here.

CSLIP compressed headers
CSLIP is a slightly more efficient version of SLIP. If you see this question, you should probably answer 'y' since you will want to use CSLIP instead of SLIP under many circumstances.

16 channels instead of 4
Normally Linux only supports 4 simultaneous SLIP connections. If you wish to have more, answer 'y' here to support up to 16. If you need more than 16 simultaneous SLIP connections, you will probably need to change some constants in the kernel source (see '`/usr/src/linux/drivers/net/slip.h`').

PPP (point-to-point) support
The Point to Point Protocol (PPP) is a slightly more generalized version of SLIP which supports more protocols and works in a wider variety of situations. For the time being, if you don't need any of the special features of PPP, CLSIP is probably a better choice; however, as modems become faster, the additional overhead of PPP will become less relevant and it will become the protocol of choice. Answer 'y' here if you need to use PPP.

PLIP (parallel port) support
Parallel Line Internet Protocol (PLIP) is a way of connecting two PCs together via their parallel ports. It is fast, but also

CPU intensive and can interfere with the use of a printer. If you wish to connect your Linux box to another PC using their parallel ports, answer 'y'.

Do you want to be offered ALPHA test drivers
: Answer 'y' to this question if you have a network device whose driver is currently under ALPHA testing and you are willing to use it even though it may crash your system and cause other problems. Currently the drivers under ALPHA testing are the 3c505, 3c50, Arcnet, AT1700, EtherExpress, NI5210, NI6510, WaveLAN, and the EISA 3200.

Western Digital/SMC cards
: If you have a Western Digital or SMC ethernet card, you should answer 'y' to this question.

*WD80*3 support*
: If you have a wd8003, wd8013, or compatible ethernet card, answer 'y' to this question. Since SMC has purchased Western Digital's networking division, many SMC ethernet cards use this driver.

SMC Ultra support
: If you have an SMC Ultra ethernet card, you should answer 'y' to this question.

AMD Lance and PCnet (AT1500 and NE2100) support
: If you have an ethernet card with one of the mentioned chipsets, such as an NE2100 or an AT1500, answer 'y' here.

3COM cards
: If you have an ethernet card made by 3COM, you should answer 'y' here.

3c501 support
: The 3c501 ethernet card has been found to be unreliable in any multitasking environment. It is strongly recommended that this card not be used under Linux. An inexpensive ne2000 clone is a good option for more reliability and throughput. If you must use the 3c501, answer 'y' here.

3c503 support.
: If you have a 3c503 ethernet card, answer 'y' here.

3c505 support
: If you have a 3c505 ethernet card, answer 'y' here.

3c507 support
: If you have a 3c507 ethernet card, answer 'y' here.

3c509/3c579 support
If you have either a 3c509 or 3c579 ethernet card, answer 'y' here.

Other ISA cards
If you have one of Cabletron E2100, DEPCA, EtherWorks3, AT1700, EtherExpress, NI5210, NI6510, HP PCLAN, HP PCLAN+, NE2000, NE1000, or an SK_G16 ethernet card, or an Arcnet or WaveLAN card, answer 'y' here.

Cabletron E21xx support
If you have a Cabletron 2100 series ethernet card, answer 'y' here.

DEPCA support
If you have a DEPCA ethernet card, answer 'y' here.

EtherWorks 3 support
If you have an EtherWorks 3 ethernet card, answer 'y' here.

Arcnet support
If you have an Arcnet card, you should answer 'y' here. However considering the speed advantages of ethernet, you should consider upgrading. The driver is still considered to be in ALPHA test.

AT1700 support
If you have an AT1700 ethernet card, answer 'y' here. The AT1700 driver is still considered to be in ALPHA test.

EtherExpress support
If you have an Intel EtherExpress ethernet card, answer 'y' here. The driver is still considered to be in ALPHA test.

NI5210 If you have an NI5210 ethernet card answer 'y' here. The driver is still considered to be in ALPHA test.

NI6510 If you have an NI6510 ethernet card answer 'y' here. The driver is still considered to be in ALPHA test.

WaveLAN support
If you have a WaveLAN card, answer 'y' here. The driver is still considered to be in ALPHA test.

HP PCLAN+ (27247B and 27252A) support
If you have an HP PCLAN plus ethernet card, answer 'y' here. These cards were sold under several model numbers, most often 2724.

HP PCLAN (27245 and other 27xxx series) support
: If you have an HP PCLAN ethernet card answer 'y' here. Most of these ethernet cards were sold with a 5 digit model number beginning with 27.

NE2000/NE1000 support
: If you have an NE2000, NE1000, or one of its many clones you should answer 'y' here.

SK_G16 support
: If you have a Schneider and Koch SK_G16 ethernet card, answer 'y' here. There are some compile time parameters in '`/usr/src/linux/drivers/net/sk_g16.c`' which you may wish to examine.

EISA, VLB, PCI and on board controllers
: If you have an Apricot Xen-II on board ethernet, a DE425, DE 434, DE435, Ansel EISA 3200, or a Zenith Z-Note, answer 'y' to this.

Ansel Communications EISA 3200 support
: If you have an Ansel Communications EISA 3200 ethernet card answer 'y' here. This driver is considered to be in ALPHA test.

Apricot Xen-II on board ethernet
: If you have an Apricot Xen-II with ethernet on the mother board, answer 'y' here.

DE425, DE434, DE435 support
: If you have one of the Digital Equipment Corporation series of EtherWORKS ethernet cards, such as the DE425, DE434, DE435, or DE500, answer 'y' here.

Zenith Z-Note support
: If you have a Zenith Z-Note with built-in ethernet based on the i82593 answer 'y' here.

Pocket and portable adaptors
: If you have an AT-LAN-TEC/RealTek pocket adapter, a D-LINK DE600 or DE620 pocket adapter answer 'y' here. For PCMCIA ethernet cards, see the PCMICA section.

AT-LAN-TEC/RealTek pocket adaptor support
: The RealTek pocket adaptor has been sold under many names. If you have a pocket adaptor which was not made by D-LINK, this driver is currently your only chance to get Linux to work with it. If you have a pocket adaptor you may wish to answer 'y' here in hopes that the driver will function. However, many pocket ethernet adaptors will never work with Linux since the

manufacturers do not believe in free software, and require non-disclosure agreements before releasing any information about their adaptors.

D-Link DE600 Pocket adaptor support
If you have a D-Link DE600 pocket ethernet adaptor answer 'y' here.

D-Link DE620 Pocket adaptor support
If you have a D-Link DE620 pocket ethernet adaptor answer 'y' here.

Sony CDU31A/CDU33A CD-ROM driver support
If you have a Sony CDU31A (single speed) or CDU33A (double speed) CD-ROM answer 'y' here. This driver is not for the newer Sony drives which are EIDE, nor for the Sony CUD535. Please be aware that many CDU31A's have a calibration problem and are unable to read the outer tracks on a CD-ROM.

Mitsumi (not IDE/ATAPI) CD-ROM driver support
If you have an older Mitsumi double speed or single speed CD-ROM, you should answer 'y' here. This driver is not for the newer Mitsumi drives such as the quad speed, which is ATAPI.

Matsushita/Panasonic CD-ROM driver support
Many CD-ROMS which use a proprietary interface are supported by this driver. If your CD-ROM is Sound Blaster compatible, it may be supported by this driver. Several CD-ROM manufacturers make drives which plug into a Sound Blaster interface, but require a special driver. These drives are *not* supported under Linux. Currently the Teac 55A is the most notable of these drives. A driver for it is in the testing stages.

LMS/Philips CD-ROM driver support
This driver is for many, but not all, Philips and LMS CD-ROM drives. There are still several older drives which will probably never be supported.

MSCDEX CD-ROM support
This driver uses 16 bit BIOS callbacks to access CD-ROM drives that would otherwise be unusable under Linux. To use this driver requires booting a special kernel after loading a minimal DOS system, and we do not recommend using it. For more information see the section on BIOS callback support. Answer 'n' here.

Matsushita/Panasonic second CD-ROM controller support
If you have more than one Matsushita/Panasonic controller, you should answer 'y' here. In general you should answer 'n' since

answering 'y' will cause a second entire copy of the driver to be loaded into memory wasting a lot of space.

Matsushita/Panasonic third CD-ROM controller support
: If you have more than two Matsushita/Panasonic controller, you should answer 'y' here. In general you should answer 'n' since answering 'y' will cause a second entire copy of the driver to be loaded into memory wasting a lot of space.

Matsushita/Panasonic fourth CD-ROM controller support
: If you have more than three Matsushita/Panasonic controller, you should answer 'y' here. In general you should answer 'n' since answering 'y' will cause a second entire copy of the driver to be loaded into memory wasting a lot of space.

Aztech/Orchid/Okano/Wearnes (non IDE) CD-ROM support
: If you have a CD-ROM drive which is not EIDE from one of the listed manufacturers, answer 'y' here.

Sony CDU535 CD-ROM driver support
: If you have a Sony CDU535 drive answer 'y' here.

Standard (minix) fs support
: This is the original Linux file system, which is compatible with the Minix file system and has 14 character file name restrictions and other limitations. It does have application to floppies. In general you should answer 'n' here unless you have a specific need for the Minix file system.

Extended fs support
: The original extended file system was written to overcome the limitations of the Minix file system. While it was quite popular for a time, there is very little reason to use it today. Answer 'n' here.

Second extended fs support
: Using his experience from writing the extended file systems, Remy Card created the second extended file system. This file system addresses the problems of the extended file system while including many new features and is designed with expandability in mind. This file system is by far the best for Linux and is comparable to all other major file systems in speed and flexibility. Answer 'y' here.

xiafs filesystem support
: The xiafs file system was a short term solution to some of the problems with the Minix file system. It is basically the Minix file system with longer file names. There is little reason to use it today. Answer 'n' here.

msdos fs support
: Answer 'y' here if you wish to be able to mount MSDOS disks under Linux. This is convenient even though you can access MSDOS disks without mounting them by using mtools. You must answer 'y' here if you wish to be able to use the UMSDOS file system.

umsdos: Unix-like fs on top of std MSDOS FAT fs
: This allows you to pretend that an MSDOS file system has features like long file names and symbolic links. Older versions have been known to cause data loss and we recommend against using it; however, if you installed Plug and Play Linux from DOS, you must answer 'y' here. Otherwise you should answer 'n'.

/proc filesystem support
: The proc file system is a means of communicating information about the kernel to user processes. If you do not answer 'y' here, standard commands like 'ps' will not function correctly.

NFS filesystem support
: If you plan on using the Network File System (NFS) you should answer 'y' here. NFS allows you to share files across the network by mounting portions of a remote file system onto your local file system.

Iso-9660 cdrom filesystem support
: Answer 'y' here, to be able to read standard CD-ROMS.

OS/2 HPFS filesystem support (read only)
: If you have an OS/2 HPFS partition on your hard drive, answer 'y' here and you will be able to read it, but not write to it from Linux.

'System V and Coherent Filesystem support'
: If you have System V or Coherent installed on your system, and wish to access the files, answer 'y' here. Many System V floppies leave the first track blank, and start the filesystem on the second. You may have trouble reading these floppies under Linux.

Cyclades async mux support
: If you have a Cyclades multiport serial card answer 'y' here.

Parallel printer support
: If you have a printer connected to your parallel port, answer 'y' here. Be aware that the printer driver often conflicts with PLIP.

Logitech busmouse support
: If you have a Logitech busmouse (not a serial mouse) answer 'y' here.

PS/2 mouse (aka "auxiliary device") support
: If you have a PS/2 style mouse, answer 'y' here. Most of the keyboard mice with the stub between the 'H' and 'J' keys are PS/2 style mice.

C&T 82C710 mouse port support (as on TI Travelmate)
: Several laptops, including the TI Travelmate, use this type of mouse port. If you have one of these, answer 'y'.

Microsoft busmouse support
: If you have a Microsoft busmouse (not a serial mouse) answer 'y' here.

ATIXL busmouse support
: Includes some older ATI video cards with a mouse port built in. If you have one of these, answer 'y'.

JMouse
: The JMouse is a mouse built into the J-Key on a keyboard, not a separate stub between the 'H' and 'J' keys. If you have one of these keyboards, answer 'y' here.

QIC-O2 tape support
: If you have a tape which uses a QIC-O2 controller, not a SCSI tape or a floppy tape, answer 'y' here.

Do you want runtime configuration for QIC-O2
: It is probably better to answer 'n' here and edit the file '`/usr/src/linux/include/linux/tpqic02.h`'. However you may wish to answer 'y' here to help you find the correct parameters for your controller.

QIC-117 tape support
: Answer 'y' if you wish to support the floppy tape module.

number of ftape buffers
: This tells the kernel how much memory to reserve for the ftape driver. If you increase this number you should get better performance from your tape at the cost of less memory available. The default value of 3 should be sufficient for most needs.

Sound card support
: If you have a supported sound card and wish to use it under Linux, you should answer 'y' here. You will be prompted for specific information about your sound card later.

PC-Speaker and DAC driver support
: If you wish Linux to attempt to emulate a sound card with the PC speaker answer 'y' here.

Kernel profiling support
: Answer 'n' here. This is only for people who are actively trying to optimize the Linux kernel. Answering 'y' here substantially

increases the amount of memory the kernel uses and slightly decreases its performance.

Remote kernel debugger
: The remote kernel debugger allows the use of GDB over a serial line on the Linux kernel. It is only for people who are actively trying to debug the kernel and have two machines connected via serial cables. Answer 'n' here.

Local kernel debugger
: The local kernel debugger is currently broken. Answer 'n' here.

Verbose SCSI error reporting (kernel size +=12K)
: If you answer 'y' here, any errors reported from the SCSI subsystem will provide more information. You should answer 'n' here unless you are having problems with your SCSI hardware and wish to know more about what is happening.

After doing the `make config` and answering all the questions you must type `make dep; make clean` to be sure all your changes take effect.

5.2 Building the Kernel

Once you have configured the kernel \refConfiguring the Kernel, you need only type

```
make zImage
```

to rebuild it. If you get errors, reconfigure the kernel and do not include any experimental drivers; also try to include only the minimum set of drivers you need to boot.

5.3 Installing the Kernel

In most circumstances, installing your new kernel is as easy as typing

```
make install
```

However, if you are using a boot floppy, then you need to copy the kernel to floppy. The easiest way to do this is to insert a formatted floppy into your `A` drive and type

```
make install
makebootfloppy
```

5.4 Kernel Modules

Linux has loadable kernel modules to add features and device driver support at run time, rather than at compile time. Kernel modules are unfortunately kernel version specific. *Every* time you build a new kernel, you must rebuild all the modules you wish to use. Many of the drivers in the kernel can be turned into loadable modules by typing

```
make modules
```

immediately after building a new kernel.

Other loadable modules such as the ftape driver and PCMCIA drivers come as separate packages in the source tree. To use these with your new kernel, you will have to recompile them as well.

5.4.1 Installing Module Source from the CD

Before you can recompile any source code, you must first put it on your hard drive. The easiest way to do this is with the control panel. See Section 5.5 [installing optional components], page 52. While running X, `su`, to root and type `control-panel`. Then click on "install source" and follow the instructions on unmounting and mounting the CD. Then click on the name of the component whose source you wish to install. If you do not wish to use the `control-panel`, you can use the either `install_component` which will copy an entire component from your CD-ROM to your hard drive or `install_path` which installs an entire directory hierarchy onto your hard drive.

To install the 'pcmcia' source code with `install_component` you must type the following commands

```
mount /dev/cdrom /system_cd/usr/src
install_component pcmcia-source
```

The `mount` command (Chapter 14 [filesystems and mounting], page 89), attaches the source CD to your file system at '/system_cd/usr/src'. You should replace '/dev/cdrom' in the above example with the device name for your CD.[1] If you have only one CD-ROM drive, you will have to make sure that the current CD is unmounted before you remove it and insert the source CD.

To install pcmcia sources from '/usr/src/device_control/pcmcia-cs-2.4.2' with `install_path`, you would put the Plug and Play Source Tree CD-ROM into a CD-ROM drive and type the following commands

```
mount /dev/cdrom /system_cd/usr/src
install_path -n /system_cd/usr/src/device_control/pcmcia-cs-2.4.2
```

Normally the `install_path` command will leave symlinks on the hard drive pointing to everything which has not yet been installed on it. The `-n` option tells `install_path` not to do this. If you wish it to appear to have

---

[1] The Plug and Play install procedure creates a symbolic link from '/dev/cdrom' to the CD-ROM device from which the system was installed, but only if you installed using a CD-ROM under Linux, and not via NFS, MS-DOS, or any other method.

symlinks back to the Plug and Play source CD, leave off the `-n` option. To learn more about `install_path` Section 5.5 [installing optional components], page 52 or type

```
man install_path
```

5.4.2 Recompiling a Module

Once you have a module's source code copied onto your hard drive, recompiling and installing it should be as easy as typing

```
make all
make install
```

If you have problems, you should check the appropriate HOWTO (which should be located in '`/usr/doc/howto`') and also look for any '`README`' files in the source directory.

5.5 Installing Optional Components

At this point you should have a working Linux system, but it will be slow and there may be commands that do not work. This is because so far only a small runtime system has been installed; the rest is still on the CD, and running from there.

If you can mount your CD under Linux, then installing the rest of the system is as easy as a few mouse clicks. If you cannot mount your CD, then you will have to install the optional components from within DOS.

If you wish to install all the binaries from the CD and you have enough space free in the appropriate places (See Chapter 14 [filesystems and mounting], page 89.) then you can install everything by logging in as root and typing

```
install_path /system_cd/usr
```

This will copy everything in /system_cd/usr from the CD-ROM onto your hard drive. This command can take up to several hours to execute, depending on the speed of your hardware.

A preferable method is to install just what you are going to use. Plug and Play Linux supports four different methods for doing this under Linux and one method under DOS (See Section 2.7.2 [dos install], page 23.)

Under Linux you may use the `control-panel`, `xfm` (See Section 5.5.2 [installing with xfm], page 55.), `install_component`, and `install_path`. The `control-panel` selection "Optional software packages" is really an X front end to `install_component`. The "Install Path" icon in root's "Applications" window lets you drag and drop files or entire directory hierarchies from your CD-ROM onto your hard drive. `install_component` lets you install components from the command line, and **install_path** lets you install files or directory hierarchies from the command line.

5.5.1 TK Install

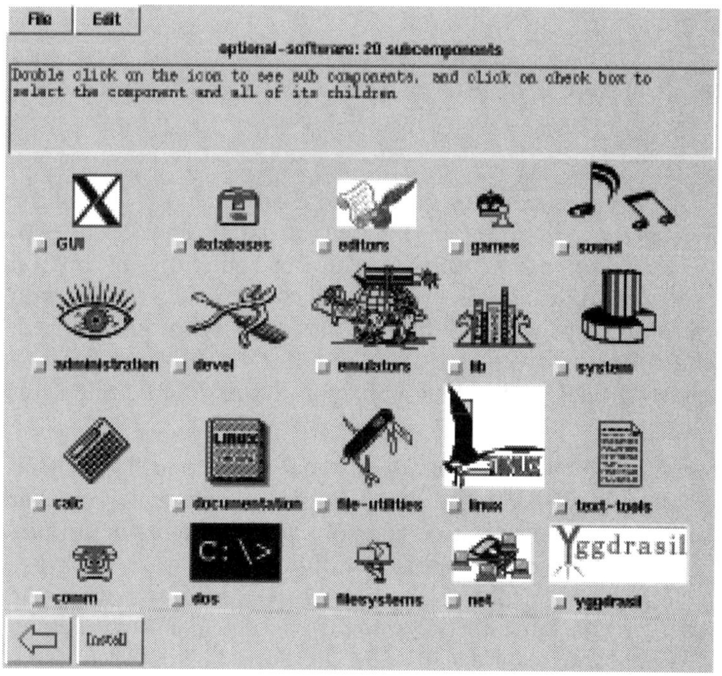

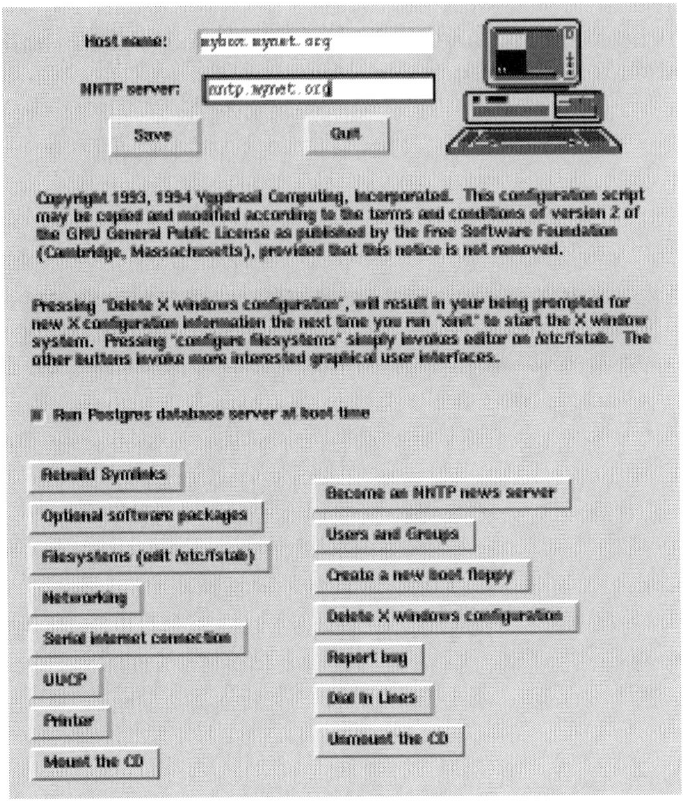

To use the `control-panel` to install software onto your hard drive, you must first be running X and be logged in as root. If the control-panel is not already on your screen type

```
control-panel&
```

in any xterm, or if you are running xfm (See Section 5.5.2 [installing with xfm], page 55), just double click on the control-panel icon in the Applications Window. Once the control panel is running, click on the button labelled "Optional software packages". When this button is pressed, you are presented with a window of icons. These icons represent a grouping of similar software. The software group name is listed at the bottom of each icon with a checkbox. Checking this box will install the software in that group.

To allow you finer control over the software that gets installed within each group, you can double-click on the icon. This will bring up another window with an icon representing each of the software packages contained within that group. You can select or deselect individual software packages within the group by checking on or off the checkbox associated with the software package. You can go back to the software group icons by clicking on the arrow icon. When you want to install, click on the install button.

This will install all the selected software. When you want to exit, select exit from the File menu.

5.5.2 Installing with XFM

You can also install optional software from within the X File Manager (See Section 5.5.2 [installing with xfm], page 55.) To install a single file or an entire directory hierarchy simply drag the file or directory icon onto the install path icon and drop it; `install_path` will do the rest. For example to install everything not in the base system from the CD onto your hard drive, first make sure the the Plug and Play CD is mounted on '`/system_cd`' and then select "Go to.." from the Folder menu and enter /system_cd for a path. Notice that the pointer must be over the entry widget for you to type anything.

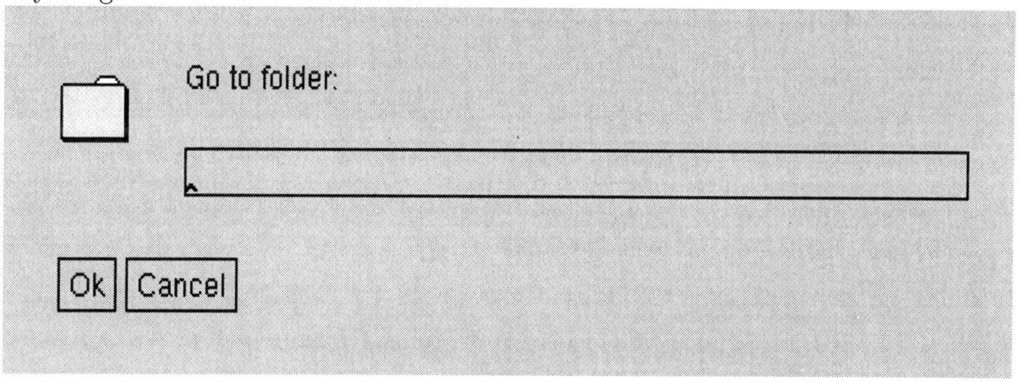

Now put the pointer on the folder marked "usr" and hold down button 1. While still holding down button 1 move the pointer to the applications window. Notice that the pointer is now a folder; that is, it has become the icon for what you are dragging. Now place the pointer over the install_path icon and release button 1.

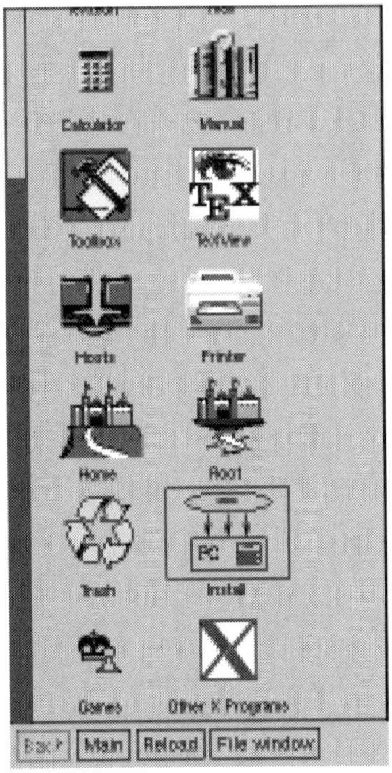

Depending on how much you choose to install, and the speed of your system, it can take several hours for such an installation to complete. While the installation is in progress, your system will be in some sort of intermediate state and may not work as you expect. In the event you have to stop the installation in the middle, or if there is a power outage, when you reboot your system will still be in an intermediate state. If this happens, make sure that the Plug and Play CD-ROM is mounted on '`/system_cd`', log in as root and type

```
/system_cd/usr/bin/perl /bin/rebuild_symlinks -s /system_cd
/system_cd / usr
```

and the system will be reset to run from the CD everything which is not already installed on the hard drive. After `rebuild_symlinks` finishes, the system should again work as expected.

5.5.3 Installing with install_component

If you do not wish to run X in order to install the optional software packages, you can do so from the command line with the `install_component` command. Install component takes as its arguments a list of packages that you wish installed. For example, to install all of the X window system, you would type

```
install_component X11
```

while logged in as root, after making sure that the Plug and Play CD-ROM is mounted on /system_cd. See Section 5.5.2 [installing with xfm], page 55, for instructions on what to do if you suffer a power failure or other problem during the install.

5.5.4 Installing with install_path

The fourth method for installing optional software packages is with the command **install_path**. **install_path** takes as its argument a single file or directory name. It then installs that file or directory hierarchy. For example to install everything on the Plug and Play CD onto your hard drive you could log in as root, make sure the Plug and Play CD is mounted on '/system_cd' and then type

```
install_path /system_cd/usr
```

When the prompt returns, the entire contents of the Plug and Play CD will be on your hard drive.

5.6 Removing Optional Components

Because some files are used by more than one software component, there is currently no perfectly correct way to remove individual software components. However, you can get a list of the files and directories associated with a base component (i.e., a component that has no children), and delete those files. The list of files associated with a component is stored on the CDROM in usr/lib/yggdrasil/components/*component*.include. For example, the file /usr/lib/yggdrasil/components/pine.include contains:

```
/usr/bin/pine
/usr/man/man1/pine.1
```

If the base component does not share files with any other base component, you can delete all of files associated with that component with the following command, assuming that you have the Plug-and-Play CDROM mounted on '/system_cd':

```
rm -rf `cat /system_cd/usr/lib/yggdrasil/components/component.include`
```

If there are shared files, you may want to look at the contents of the file *component*.include, and only files that are not shared or delete all of the files associated with the component as shown in the preceding command, and then reinstall the components that share files with the component that you have deleted. You can find what other components include a file or directory with a command like:

```
egrep file_you_are_looking_for \
     /system_cd/usr/lib/yggdrasil/components/*.include
```

6 The Control Panel

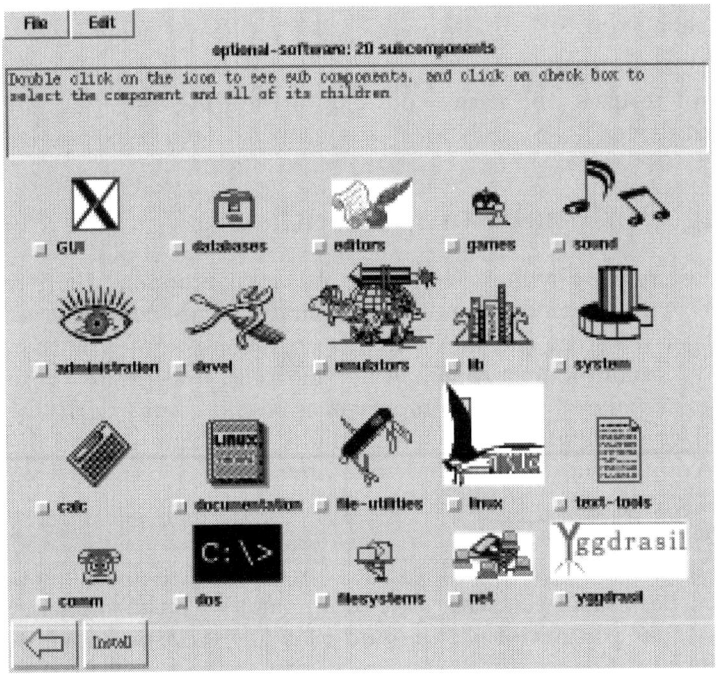

The `control-panel` is a graphical means of installing and configuring software. You must be logged in as root and in X to be able to use the `control-panel`. To bring it up , you enter `control-panel &` in an xterm window or you can select `Control Panel` in the X Utilities pop-up menu.

The following is a list of control panels brought up when their appropriate buttons are clicked on.

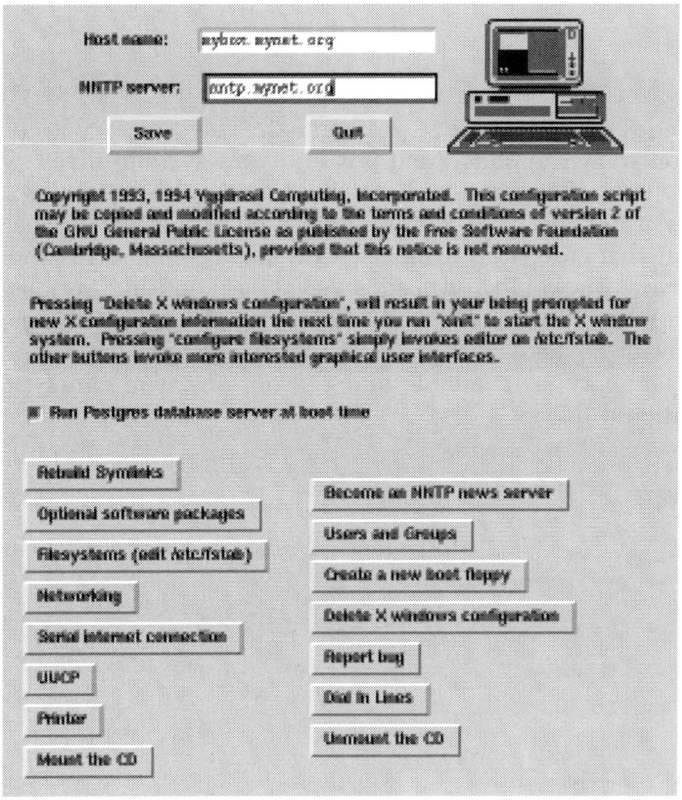

Optional Software

When this button is pressed, you are presented with a window of icons, each of which represents a group of similar software. The software group name is listed at the bottom of each icon, along with a checkbox. Checking this box will install all the software in that group. To allow you finer control over the software that gets installed as a part of each group, you can double-click on its icon. This will bring up another window with an icon representing each of the software packages contained within the group. You can select or deselect individual software packages within the group by checking on or off the checkboxes associated with the software packages. When you have finished, return to the software group icons by clicking on the arrow icon. When you want to install, click on the install button. This will install all the selected software. When you want to exit, select exit from the File menu.

Filesystems (Edit /etc/fstab)

When this button is pressed, you are presented with the vi editor with which you can add, delete, or edit the entries in your /etc/fstab file. Each line in the /etc/fstab file represents a file system that you want mounted on boot. The format for each line in the file is:

device directory fstype options

For example,

/dev/sda1 /home ext2 defaults

The device (/dev/sda1) is what you want mounted. The directory is the mount point where you want the file system put into your system directory tree; this can be anywhere. You can use the mkdir command to add a new mount point directory if desired. The fstype is the type of file system that you wish to mount; in this case, it is a linux (ext2) file system. If it were an MS-DOS file system, you would use msdos. Next is mounting options, for example ro for read-only. In the example above, defaults means for the ext2 file system, we want to read and write to the file system. For more information on file system types available and the options, you can type man fstab at the command line.

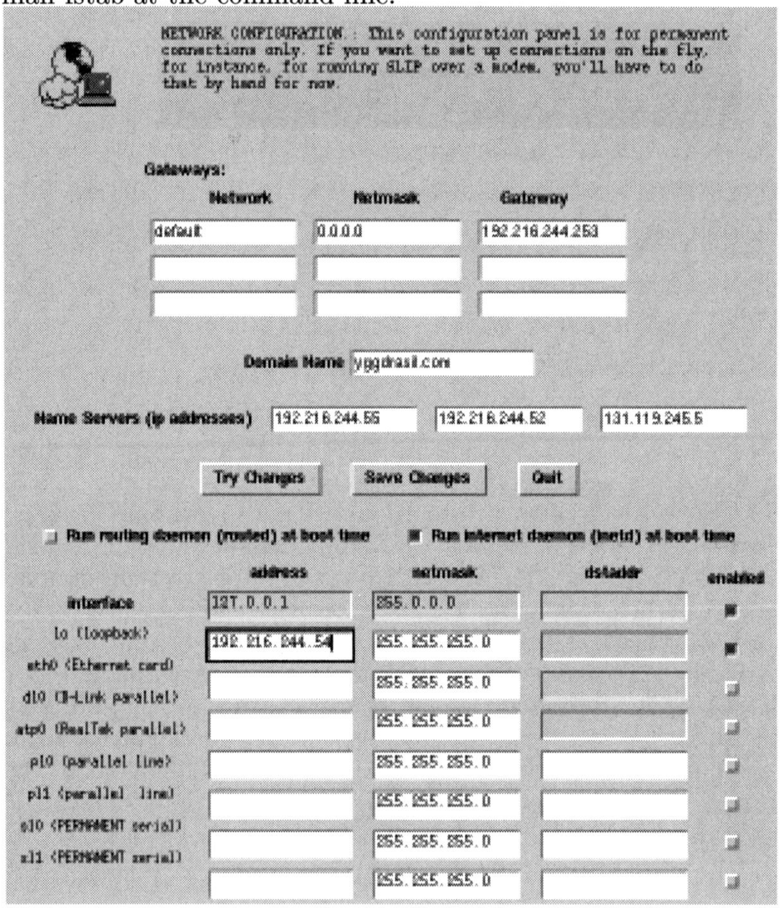

Networking

When this button is pressed, you are presented with a control panel that will set your networking configuration files. This control panel is to be used for permanent connections only; there is a separate control panel for doing SLIP connections. You need to have specific information available for setting up networking. Specifically, you will need to know your machine's domain name, IP address, and netmask. In addition, you will need to know gateway names and netmasks, and name server IP addresses. This information is all used to configure DNS. You can also choose to start the routing daemon (routed) and the internet daemon (inetd) at boot time. This will put the appropriate entries in the /etc/rc.d directory. For example:

```
If you have a gateway, you would fill in the network, netmask, and
gateway entries at the top of the form. For example:

default 0.0.0.0 191.205.244.222

You should fill in the domain name; this is the domain of your
network. For example, the Yggdrasil domain name is: yggdrasil.com

If you know the IP addresses of name servers that you can use, put them
in the Name Servers boxes. You can enter the IP addresses of up to three
name servers.

If you want to run the routing daemon (routed) or the internet daemon
(inetd) at boot time, check the appropriate boxes.

The rest of the form concerns itself with filling in the IP address,
netmask, and dst addresses of the networking hardware for your
machine. Notice that the loopback line is already filled in for you with
the standard loopback interface IP address of 127.0.0.1. The rest of the
form needs to be filled in with the appropriate information for each
interface available. For example, if you have a single ethernet card in
your machine, you would fill in the eth0 line with something like the
following:

192.205.24.21 255.255.255.0

and insure that the enabled checkbox is checked.
```

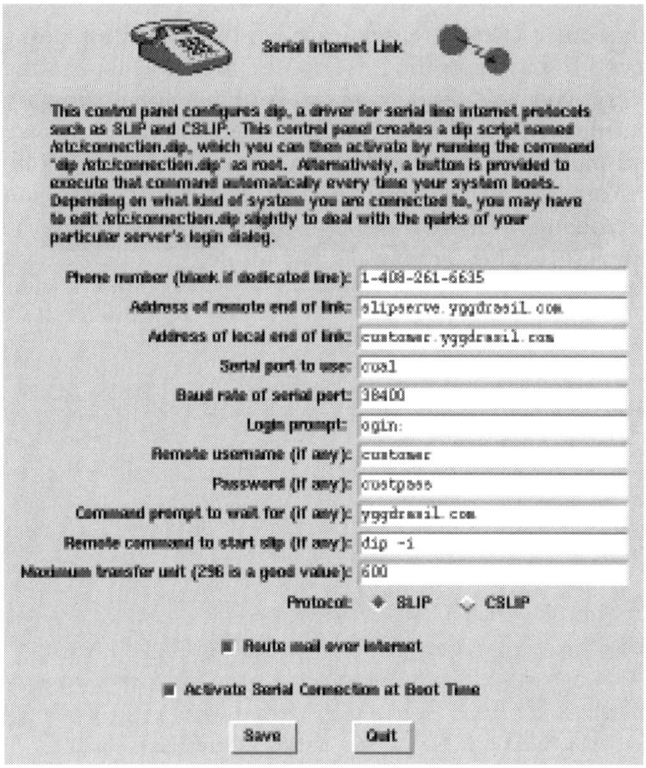

Serial Internet Connection

When this button is pressed, you are presented with a control panel that will set up a dip script for a SLIP connection with a statically assigned IP address. The script will be saved as /etc/connection.dip. Simply supply the information requested in the control panel to have the script automatically generated for you. The control panel can optionally enable the script to be run at boot time by creating an entry in /etc/rc.d. More information can be obtained by typing man dip at the command line. Here is an example of how to fill in this form:

```
Fill in the phone number of the SLIP provider; this may be your internet
provider. Then fill in the IP address of the remote end of the link. If
you have a name server running you can fill in its name instead
(e.g. shell.foo.com). Next, fill in the IP address designated for your
machine (e.g. todo.foo.com). Then specify which serial port you are
using for SLIP. This will be cua0, cua1, cua2, or cua3. These correspond
to COM1 through COM4. Then specify the baud rate of the serial port
(e.g. 38400). Next fill in a string that the remote computer host will
send when you are connected (e.g. login:). Next, provide your user login
name, your password, a command prompt to wait for, the command to start
slip (e.g. dip -i), and the maximum transfer unit size. Select the SLIP
or CSLIP option. Elect to route mail over the internet and whether you
want to activate the SLIP connection at boot. This will automatically
```

```
dial in to your SLIP provider at boot time.
```

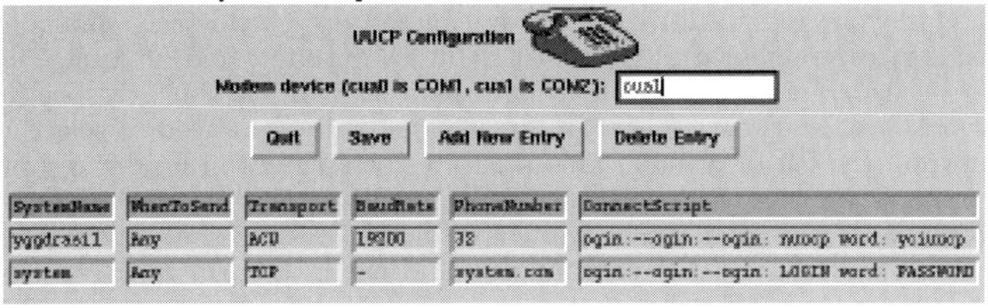

UUCP

When this button is pressed, you are presented with a control panel with which to set up the UUCP configuration files. Setting up UUCP can be complex and any good book on UUCP can be of help. Also, more information can be had by typing man uucp at the command line. You must specify what modem device you are using for the UUCP connection. This will be cua0 through cua3 which corresponds to COM1 through COM4. Here is an example of an entry in the UUCP configuration dialog:

```
foo Any ACU 19200 444-4444 login:--login:--login:LOGIN word: PASSWORD
```

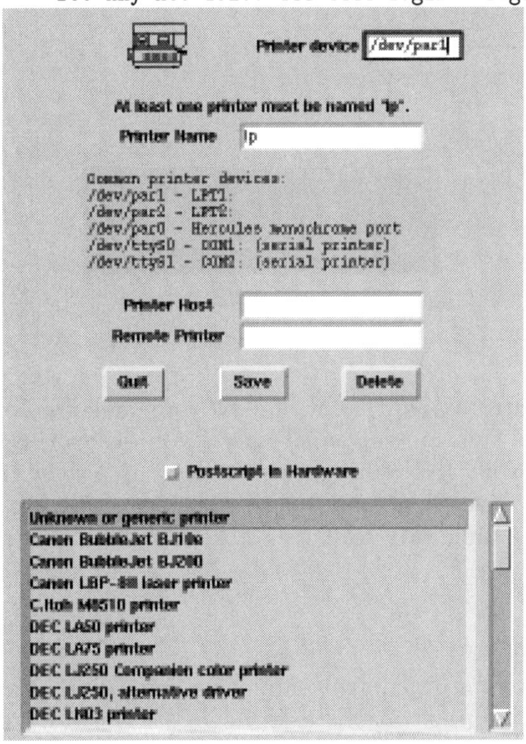

Printer

When this button is pressed, you are presented with control panel used to configure your /etc/printcap file. Simply enter a printer device (common printer devices are shown). You must name the printer, and at least one printer needs to be named lp. If using a network printer, you can specify the printer host and remote host information. Finally, you need to select a printer from the list of printers presented. If Postscript is in hardware (on your printer) you need to check on the Postscript in Hardware checkbox. For example, if you have a parallel printer on LPT1, you would fill in the Printer device entry as /dev/par1. You would name the printer lp. If you want to use a remote printer on the network, you would enter the host name and then the printer name available on that host. Next, you would enable the Postscript In Hardware checkbox if appropriate. Next, you would select your printer from the list of printers. Then you would click on Save and then Quit. This will configure the appropriate files for you (e.g. /etc/printcap).

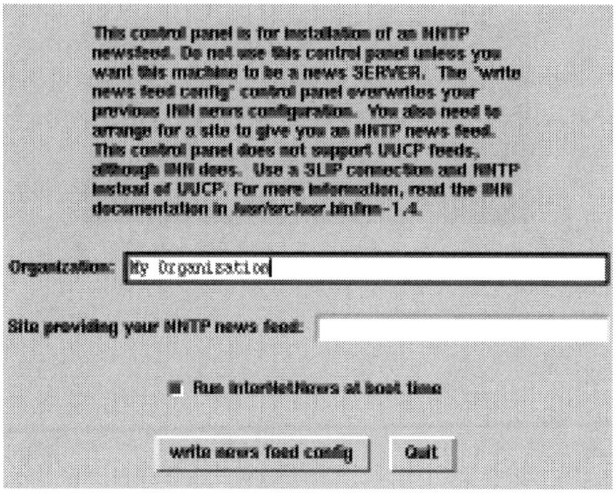

Become an NNTP News Server

This button will bring up a control panel that will allow your machine to become a news server. Do not use this control panel unless you desire this. This control panel will overwrite your INN configuration files. Also, it will not work with UUCP news feeds; use SLIP and NNTP instead of UUCP. For more information, read the documentation in /usr/src/usr.bin/inn-1.4.

Users and Groups

When pressed, this button brings up a control panel that will allow you to graphically do typical system administration tasks normally performed on the /etc/passwd file (providing you have permission to do that), such as add, delete, edit user's information, etc.

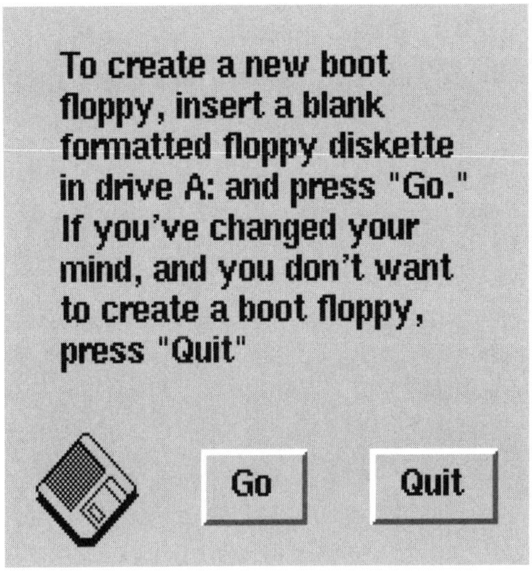

Create A New Boot Floppy

Pressing this button will bring up a control panel that will allow you to create a new boot floppy on /dev/fd0 (drive A: in MS-DOS). You also have the option of not creating a boot floppy if you change your mind.

Delete X Windows Configuration

Pressing this button will delete your /var/lib/X11 X configuration files. By doing this, the next time you run xinit from the command line, you will be prompted for new X configuration information.

Report Bug

If you have your machine already set up to send mail through the internet, you can report bugs by filling in this form, but you cannot be logged in as root to use this mechanism.

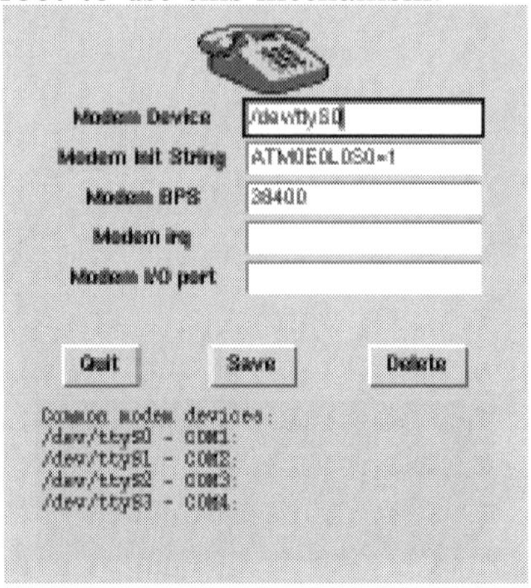

Dial In Lines

Pressing this button will bring up a control panel that will allow configuration of your /etc/initab and support files to enable your machine to handle incoming dial-in connections. For example, fill in the correct modem device (e.g. /dev/ttyS0), a modem initialization string (e.g. ATM0E0L0S0-1), the modem baud rate (e.g. 38400), the IRQ of the modem (e.g. 5), and the I/O port of the modem (e.g. 0xCE00).

Unmount the CD

Will simply unmount your CD-ROM. If a process is preventing unmounting the CD, a window will pop up and show the process(es) that are using the CD-ROM. You are then able to click on the process(es) to send them signals to shut down, after which you will be able to umount the CD-ROM.

7 Interesting Features

This chapter exists to point out a few of the more interesting features of Plug-and-Play Linux. This chapter is not essential reading. You can come back and browse it later.

7.1 xfm

Xfm is a file and applications manager program for the X window system. It provides virtually all of the features that you would expect in a file manager — move around your directory tree in multiple windows, move, copy or delete files, and launch programs with simple mouse operations. Directory displays are updated automatically at regular intervals when the contents of the directory changes. The integrated application manager provides a kind of shelf onto which you can place your favorite applications, as well as the files and directories you are currently using. It also allows you to access different groups of applications and files. User-definable file types let you specify a command to be executed when double-clicking on a file or dropping other files onto it. Last but not least, xfm can automatically mount and unmount special devices like floppies as you open and close the corresponding directories (mount points).

7.2 The Andrew System

The Andrew System is a multimedia system, consisting of applications and a toolkit. The most useful application is `ez`, an editor for easy creation and reading of documents with embedded images, equations, spreadsheets, hypertext links, and many other media types. When you're running X windows, `ez /usr/packages/andrew/doc/AtkTour/Media` will invoke the `ez` editor with a file that shows most of the built-in Andrew media types. This file is part of a tour of the Andrew system, which you can access with the command `ez /usr/packages/andrew/doc/AtkTour/Tour`. You can get topic-specific help on andrew with the `/usr/packages/andrew/bin/help` command. Note that you have to type in the full path name, because the command '`help`' by itself will invoke the help function that is built into the Bourne Again Shell. Finally, try `/usr/packages/andrew/bin/messages` to send and receive multimedia mail. `messages` reads mail in a format that is slightly different from the format used by most mailers, so you can use `eatmail` to convert your spooled mail to Andrew format. Be warned that there is currently no facility for converting your mail back.

If you are running either the `fvwm` or `twm` window manager in the default configuration, then you can also invoke these commands from the menus that are displayed when you click on the root window (the root window is the background area of the screen, i.e., the area that is not covered by any other window).

7.3 Multimedia Electronic Mail

Try logging into the `guest` account and starting X-windows with the `xinit` command. Once you have X-windows running, try running `/usr/packages/andrew/bin/readmessages` to read multimedia electronic mail. The guest account and every new account that is created with the graphical control panel has an Andrew email message in its mail box that talks about how to use the Andrew system. The message contains some text, some hypertext links and a picture of Saturn. This facility is not just a spiffy looking demo; it is multimedia email software that you can use on a day-to-day basis.

7.4 Sound

By default, the kernel is configured to look for a Soundblaster-compatible sound card on IRQ 7, and a Media Vision ProAudio Spectrum 16 card on IRQ 10. As always, you have a choice between configuring your cards to match the expectations of the kernel, or rebuilding the kernel to match your cards. If you want to rebuild the kernel, note that the IRQ numbers for the sound cards are controlled by the top level Makefile (look for the string "SBC_IRQ").

You may also want to rebuild the kernel if you have a Gravis Ultrasound card or an MPU-401. The kernel source has drivers for these sound cards, but they are not configured into the standard kernel because they cause systems with certain hardware configurations to hang during the boot process. See the section "Rebuilding the Kernel" for more information on how to reconfigure and rebuild your kernel.

You can use the `splay` program to play ".snd" sound files. By default, splay plays 8-bit monophonic sound, but it has options to play stereo ("-S") and to play other 12-bit or 16-bit sound samples ("-b"). Type `splay -help` for a synopsis.

You can synthesize instrumental music with `fmplay`. Before using `fmplay`, you must load instruments onto your sound board with the `sbiset` command. The file '`/usr/packages/sound/fm/setall`' will install 128 instruments on your sound board. You may want to run '`/usr/packages/sound/fm/setall`' and then use fmplay on the sample MIDI files in '`/usr/packages/sound/fm/midifile`'.

There is also a `midplay` program which is like `fmplay`, except that it plays MIDI files directly over the MIDI interface on your sound card.

7.5 Transparent Decompression

If you compress a file with **gzip**, it creates a smaller file with a '.gz' extension. There is a facility in Plug-and-Play Linux to make the '.gz' files look like they are not compressed. When you read them, the **gunzip** decompressor is automatically invoked. The '/usr/src' source tree on the CD-ROM uses this facility. To turn on transparent decompression type:

```
export LD_PRELOAD=/usr/lib/uncompress.so.5
```

To turn off transparent decompression type:

```
unset LD_PRELOAD
```

7.6 Image Viewers

Plug-and-Play Linux includes the ImageMagic tools for manipulating images. Of particular interest is the `display` program, which can display a variety of image formats under X windows, including JPEG, GIF and many others. We include ImageMagic instead of xv because the ImageMagic software is more powerful, has better dithering algorithms and is free, while xv is shareware. Also included is Xli which is similar in display capability.

7.7 The MPEG Video Player

The MPEG video player is '/usr/bin/X11/mpeg_play'. Type `mpeg_play -help` for more information on mpeg_play and look in '~demo' for two sample MPEG files, birdisba.mpg and hulahoop.mpg.

7.8 Ghostscript: the GNU Postscript Emulator

Ghostscript is a postscript emulator that can draw to an X window, a number of printers, or to data files in a number of formats, including fax file formats. You can get a brief synopsis of how to use ghostscript and what devices are supported with the command `gs -help`. There is documentation on ghostscript in /usr/lib/ghostscript/doc.

If you want to look at postscript in an X window, check out `ghostview`, which is a program that uses ghostscript to allow you to browse a postscript file in an X window.

7.9 Tcl, Tk, Wish, and Expect

Tcl is a scripting language ("tool command language") written by Professor John Ousterhout at UC Berkeley. Tcl is accessible as a library, /usr/lib/libtcl.a, which other programs can use. The Tcl README file suggests some sources of information on Tcl:

> For an introduction to the facilities provided by Tcl, your best bet is to retrieve the partial draft of the Tcl/Tk book, which is available for FTP from the standard Tcl/Tk release directories. Another possibility is to see the paper "Tcl: An Embeddable Command Language", in the Proceedings of the 1990 Summer USENIX Conference. A copy of that paper is also available in Postscript form in the distribution directory. However, the paper corresponds to a much earlier version of Tcl (approximately version 3.0), so some details of the paper may not be correct anymore and there are many new features not described in the paper.

Tk is a toolkit that allows one to quickly write X-windows programs in Tcl. Wish is an interpreter for Tk. Using wish seems to be the typical way that people learn to use Tk and Tcl. You can invoke `wish` as a command and play with it.

You can read about Tk and wish in Professor John Ousterhout's paper, "An X11 Toolkit Based on the Tcl Language" in the Winter 1991 USENIX conference proceedings. The source code for the hypertext, barchart and graph extensions to Tk is in /usr/src/usr.bin/graph-1.0.

Getting away from X, expect is a system written in Tcl by Don Libes that "performs programmed dialogue with other interactive programs." Expect scripts in /usr/bin include archie, weather, rftp, and kibitz. The expect README file suggests some sources of information on expect:

> The implementation, philosophy, and design of expect are discussed in "expect: Curing Those Uncontrollable Fits of Interaction", Proceedings of the Summer 1990 USENIX Conference, Anaheim, CA, June 11-15, 1990. Examples and discussion, specifically aimed at system administrators, are in "Using expect to Automate System Administration Tasks", Proceedings of the 1990 USENIX Large Systems Administration Conference (LISA) IV, Colorado Springs, CO, October 17-19, 1990. A comprehensive paper of example scripts is "expect: Scripts for Controlling Interactive Programs", Computing Systems, Vol. 4, No. 2, University of California Press Journals, 1991. Regression and conformance testing is discussed in "Regression Testing and Conformance Testing Interactive Programs", Proceedings of the Summer 1992 USENIX Conference, San Antonio, TX, June 8-12, 1992. An explanation of some of the more

interesting source code to Expect itself is in Chapter 36 ("Expect") of "Obfuscated C and Other Mysteries", John Wiley & Sons, 1993. A paper on connecting multiple interactive programs together using Expect is "Kibitz - Connecting Multiple Interactive Programs Together", Software - Practice & Experience, to appear.

7.10 X Games

On this release you will find a number of games which can be played under X. The easiest way to start playing these games is if you have fvwm or twm as your window manager, you can click your mouse on the desktop and bring up the root popup menu. Under this menu, you will find a games menu item. Under the games menu item is another popup menu that will bring up the games.

`Asteroids` Asteroids is a version of the time tested arcade game. Maneuver your spacecraft through meteor fields. Avoid alien ships...

`Battle Zone (cbzone)` Cbzone is a version of Battle Zone derived from the Fortran sources written by Justin S. Revenaugh. This version is more flexible in that the number of opponents is user selectable.

Input to the the game is primarily through the mouse, although some keyboard commands are accepted. Mouse left button will fire a salvo; mouse right button will switch between low/high gear. On a three button mouse, the middle button will center the joystick and stop your tank. This can be done on a two button mouse by pressing both buttons at the same time. Directional control of the tank is achieved by moving the mouse to different portions of the screen. The joystick in the lower right hand corner of the screen will correspond to your tank's current movement and rotation.

Because of the interface between mouse position and game input, the program will attempt to create a window that covers the entire screen. Since some window managers will attempt to title and border any windows as well as let the user place them, the program will adjust the window position after the user places it anywhere on the screen. However, the first few graphic objects may not be drawn; in this case keyboard command 'r' (redraw) should resolve the problem.

`Chess (xboard)` Xboard is an X11 chessboard that can serve as a user interface for GNU Chess or for the Internet Chess Server. As an interface to GNU Chess, xboard lets you play a game against the machine, set up arbitrary positions, force variations, or watch a game between two machines. As an interface to the Internet Chess Server, xboard lets you play against other ICS users, observe games being played by others, or review games that have recently finished. You can also use xboard as a chessboard to play through games. It will read a game file or allow you to play through a variation manually. This is useful for keeping track of email postal games, browsing games off the net, or reviewing GNU Chess and ICS games you have saved.

`Connect Four (xvier)` Xvier is a board game where you and the computer alternately throw stones into free columns. The stones pile up in the columns, and the goal is to get four stones in a row, in a column, or diagonally. You can choose various board sizes and levels of difficulty.

`Lunar Lander` Try your hand at landing a lunar module on the moon.

`Mille Bornes` The traditional French card game in which you test your luck and skill against the computer on an imagined car trip. You try to gain mileage while plotting against your opponent. Your opponent will try to plot against you. You play accidents and misfortunes against one another while trying to be the first to complete the trip.

`Othello (Reve)` Reve is played on an 8 x 8 board, with stones which should be considered to be black on one side and white on the other. A legal move consists of placing a stone of one's own color on the board so as to "sandwich" one or more rows (orthogonal or diagonal) of stones of the opposite color between the stone just placed and another stone of the same color. All stones so sandwiched are flipped over to reveal the color of the other side (your own color).

The object of the game, is to have more stones than the opponent at the end of the game (i.e. when the board is full or neither side has a legal move). If you have no legal move, you simply miss a turn. Black goes first.

`Pool` If you know how to play pool, excellent; if you don't, here's your chance! With the current setup, you have two sets of balls. The first set is balls 1 through 7. The second set is balls 9 through 15. Whoever gets their balls in first and then gets the black ball in last wins. There is no automatic scoring, so whoever wins is supposed to increase their score by clicking on the proper '+' color button. If you want to see where your ball will go, click on 'Cheat' button to get a trajectory of the shot.

The cue stick length determines how hard you hit the ball, so if you want to hit harder, change your cue stick length by moving your mouse away from the white ball. You don't have to click on the white ball to start stick handling; you can click anywhere on the table. The white ball goes in the opposite direction relative to the cue stick.

`Shogi` The Japanese form of Chess.

`Solitaire (Spider)` Spider is a particularly challenging double-deck solitaire. Unlike most solitaires, it provides extraordinary opportunities for the skillful player to overcome bad luck in the deal by means of careful analysis and complex manipulations.

`Xtank` The classic xtank game allows you to play against others on your network.

7.11 Networking

Linux can easily be integrated into a TCP/IP network. Linux supports common Ethernet boards and TCP/IP connections via a modem with SLIP or PPP. This allows you to configure your Linux workstation as an FTP server, gopher server, or World Wide Web server. Linux is a fast track to the Internet.

7.12 TCP/IP, NFS, and Your Ethernet Adapter

You can configure TCP/IP networking with the `control-panel` command when you're logged in as root under X windows. To unconfigure TCP/IP, delete the file /etc/rc.net and reboot. If you are on a network running TCP/IP, you should be able to mount and unmount NFS filesystems in the same way that you would on any other workstation:

```
mount -t nfs hostname:/remotefilesystem /local_mountpoint
```

```
umount /local_mountpoint
```

7.13 Other Useful Programs

There are many other useful programs that you might want to try. For example, the TEX typesetting system (the command name is `tex`) complete with xdvi for viewing the DVI format output in an X window and dvips for converting the DVI format output to PostScript.

For telecommunications, there is cu and, for uploading, z-modem. The zmodem commands are `rz` and `sz`). If you want to use upload with zmodem, you can do so by starting the sz command on the remote machine, suspending cu (with ~ Ctrl-Z) and then running rz with its standard input and output redirected to the modem, for example:

```
rz < /dev/ttyS1 > /dev/ttyS1
```

8 Getting Help

The serial number on the inside back cover the this manual entitles you to one free use of our $25 Guaranteed Technical Support service (capped at 15 minutes), and $5 off of your second call (See Section 8.5.3 [Guaranteed Technical Support], page 81). However, it is probably worth your while to read this chapter before calling for technical support so that you don't waste your free call on something that you can easily figure out for yourself.

If you are unable to get your system running at all, then you should skip to Section 8.4 [usenet], page 79.

Once you have your system running, most of your questions will be on what commands are available and how to use them. If you are running the `bash` shell (the default), then getting a list of all available commands is as easy as pressing the Tab key twice; however, be prepared for a little wait and a long list of commands. Currently there are approximately 1500 commands available ranging from `a2p` to `zsoelim`. Now that you know how to find a list of all the commands, you are most likely asking what they all do. Under Linux there are several ways to find out what a command does.

8.1 The Man Command

The most common form of online help under Linux is the manual pages. Most commands have a manual page which gives a summary of the command and all its options. To read a manual page, use the `man` command. Perhaps the best example to give is the manual page for the `man` command. If you type

```
man man
```

at the command prompt. You should see something like

```
man(1) Manual pager utils man(1)

NAME
man - an interface to the on-line reference manuals

SYNOPSIS
man [-acdhwut7ZV] [-m system[,...]] [-L locale] [-p string] [-M path]
[-P pager] [-r prompt] [-T device] [-S list] [-e extension]
[[section] page ...] ...
man -l [-t7Z] [-p string] [-P pager] [-r prompt] [-T device] file ...
man -k [-M path] keyword ...
man -f [-M path] page ...

DESCRIPTION
man is the system's manual pager. Each page argument given to man is
normally the name of a program, utility or function. The manual page
associated with each of these arguments is then found and displayed. A
section, if provided, will direct man to look only in that section of
the manual. The default action is to search in all of the available
sections, following a pre-defined order and to show only the first page
found, even if the page exists in several sections.

The table below shows the section numbers of the manual followed by the
types of pages they contain.

1 Executable programs or shell commands
2 System calls (functions provided by the kernel)
3 Library calls (functions within system libraries)
4 Special files (usually found in /dev)
5 File formats and conventions e.g. /etc/passwd
6 Games
7 Macro packages and conventions e.g. man(7), groff(7).
8 System administration commands (usually only for root)
9 Kernel routines [only found in Linux]
n new [obsolete]
l local [obsolete]
p public [obsolete]
o old [obsolete]

A manual page consists of several parts.

They may be labelled NAME, SYNOPSIS, DESCRIPTION, OPTIONS, FILES, SEE
ALSO, BUGS, and AUTHOR.

The following conventions apply to the SYNOPSIS section Manual page
man(1)
```

This man page describes the format of the man page. In the upper corners the string "man(1)" appears. This tells you that you are reading the manual page for the `man` command and it is from section 1 of the manual.

The different sections of the manual are listed in the man page; section 1 is for executable programs or shell commands. There is also a manual page for `man` in section 7 of the manual, but this manual page has to do with writing manual pages, not reading them. To see the next page of the manual command, press the space bar. For information on moving around the man page, searching for strings, and so on, press the 'h' key.

Other manual pages which you should read are the ones for `bash`, `ls`, `cd`, and any others which catch your fancy. For a list of more than 500 manual pages in section 1, type

```
ls /usr/man/man1
```

There are more manual pages in other sections and even in section 1, stored in other directories such as '`/usr/X11/man/man1`'.

8.2 The Info Command

The man pages for several commands are incomplete and obsolete, yet refer you to something called "info". The info system is a form of documentation, made popular by the Free Software Foundation, which allows the same documentation source to be nicely typeset, and also provided online with little additional effort.

The two easiest ways to enter the info system are to type `info` on the command line or type `emacs` on the command line and then press `CONTROL-H` followed by the "i" key.

Once in the info system, press `CONTROL-H` for help on info. The movement commands are based on the cursor control keys for emacs. Pressing `CONTROL-N` moves the cursor down one line (next-line), pressing `CONTROL-P` moves the cursor up one line (previous-line), pressing `CONTROL-F` moves the cursor forward one character (forward-character), and pressing Control-b moves the cursor backwards one character (backward-character). With the cursor over a topic, press return to view the information on that topic. For example when you first run the `info` command, you should see something like

```
File: dir Node: Top This is the top of the INFO tree
This (the Directory node) gives a menu of major topics. Typing "d"
returns here, "q" exits, "?" lists all INFO commands, "h" gives a
primer for first-timers, "mTexinfo<Return>" visits Texinfo topic, etc.
--- PLEASE ADD DOCUMENTATION TO THIS TREE. (See INFO topic first.) ---

* Menu: The list of major topics begins on the next line.

-- Help on Using the Info system
* Info: (info).  Documentation browsing system.

-- Misc
* Linux FAQ: (linux-faq). Linux Frequently Asked Questions with Answers.

-- General Topics --
* Bash: (bash).  The GNU bash features guide
* Dc: (dc).  DC, an arbitrary precision calculator.
* Ed: (ed).  The 'ed' command, which has the purpose of editing
text files.
* Gzip: (gzip).  The the GNU 'gzip' command for compressing files.
* Ispell: (ispell).  ISPELL, an interactive spelling corrector
-----Info: (dir)Top, 75 lines --Top---------------------------------------
--- Welcome to Info version 2.10-p1. Type "C-h" for help.
```

The cursor will start in the upper left corner, and if you press `CONTROL-N` 10 times, it should be on the line

```
File: dir Node: Top This is the top of the INFO tree
This (the Directory node) gives a menu of major topics. Typing "d"
returns here, "q" exits, "?" lists all INFO commands, "h" gives a
primer for first-timers, "mTexinfo<Return>" visits Texinfo topic, etc.
--- PLEASE ADD DOCUMENTATION TO THIS TREE. (See INFO topic first.) ---

* Menu: The list of major topics begins on the next line.

-- Help on Using the Info system
* Info: (info).  Documentation browsing system.

-- Misc
* Linux FAQ: (linux-faq). Linux Frequently Asked Questions with Answers.

-- General Topics --
* Bash: (bash).  The GNU bash features guide
* Dc: (dc).  DC, an arbitrary precision calculator.
* Ed: (ed).  The 'ed' command, which has the purpose of editing
text files.
* Gzip: (gzip).  The the GNU 'gzip' command for compressing files.
* Ispell: (ispell).  ISPELL, an interactive spelling corrector
-----Info: (dir)Top, 75 lines --Top-----------------------------------------
--- Welcome to Info version 2.10-p1. Type "C-h" for help.
```

The cursor will start in the upper left corner, and if you press `CONTROL-N` 10 times, it should be on the line

```
* Info: (info).  Documentation browsing system.
```

Pressing return will give you information about the info system, including everything you need to know to use the info system, and even create info pages. If you wish to create your own info pages, you should purchase a copy of "Texinfo the GNU Documentation Format" from the Free Software Foundation in Cambridge, MA. Other useful info pages include the emacs info page, and the bash info page.

There is a third method for accessing info pages provided with Plug and Play Linux. The command `tkinfo` will bring up an X based info browser. Unfortunately it is far from complete and may not be usable under all circumstances.

8.3 Other Online Documentation

In the directory '`/usr/doc`', you will find several books from the Linux Documentation Project as well as other miscellaneous documentation. Much of this documentation is not in a format which is easily read; it needs to be uncompressed or read with the command `zmore`. For example to read the Linux Installation and Getting Started Guide by Matt Welsh, type

```
cd /usr/doc/install-guide-2.1.1
```

```
zmore install-guide-2.1.1.txt.gz
```

The ".gz" ending of the file above means that it has been compressed with `gzip` and the ".txt" means that it is a text file. The `zmore` command should let you examine any text file that gzip understands, including those ending in just ".Z".

Hardcopy of most of '`/usr/doc`' is available from Yggdrasil in the form of The Linux Bible. Please see the order form in the back of this manual to order.

8.4 Getting Help on the Net

Linux was developed by large groups of people cooperating on the Internet, and many of the original developers still respond to postings once in a while. There are also many knowledgeable people who read news and answer questions in their spare time, so the Net is often a good way to get help. However, there are a few rules to follow if you expect to get any useful information back.

- Read all relevant FAQ's first
- Be polite.
- Be succinct.
- Include all necessary information.

Rather than wasting other people's time and money, you should consult the relevant FAQ's first. FAQ stands for Frequently Asked Questions, and usually include answers to most problems that novices might encounter. Some of the most common problems people have with file permissions and `rm` are answered in a FAQ. The FAQs are available via anonymous FTP from rtfm.mit.edu and are posted regularly to news.answers.

If you do need to post, remember your message will be read by thousands of people world wide, many of whom are paying for the privilege of doing so. They will not appreciate insults or even practices that go against established procedure. For more complete information see the nettiquette postings in `news.newusers.announce`, but here are a few rules of thumb:

- Check your spelling.
- Do not use all caps, it is considered to be shouting.
- Include a meaningful subject and keywords lines.
- Post your message to only one relevant news group.
- Do not ask to be emailed an answer because you can't be bothered to read the group.
- Format your message for about 70 columns.

If you are too verbose people will not bother to read your entire message and you will not get any answers. On the other hand, if you do not include enough information no one will be able to understand your questions. Your message should include a brief summary of the problem with details following. Be sure to include the kernel version you are running as well as the version of libc you are using. The kernel version can be obtained by typing

```
uname -a
```

and the version of libc you are running can be obtained by typing

```
ldd /bin/ls
```

or if it is a particular program that is giving you trouble

```
ldd 'which <program name>'
```

where <program name> should be replaced with the name of the program that is giving you problems. If you are having problems with the kernel or with recognizing specific hardware, you should also include a list of all your hardware including the I/O ports, DMA channels, and IRQs that each individual hardware component is using as well as complete model names and numbers. See Chapter 9 [pc hardware], page 83.

If a program is behaving differently than you expect, you should include the exact commands you used, and the exact output you get. Then explain why you think you this output is wrong, and what benefit there would be to changing the program in question. Remember, just because your favorite un*x clone behaves a certain way, does not mean that this is the best behavior for Linux.

8.5 Commercial Support

Commercial support for Linux is available from several vendors. See Section E.1 [linux services], page 153. At Yggdrasil we offer the following support services:

- Consulting Hotline
- Guaranteed Technical Support
- Personal Technical Support Contract
- Business Technical Support Contract
- Release on Demand
- General Technical Services
- Development Contracts

8.5.1 Consulting Hotline

This service comes in two forms. The first is via a 900 number available only in the United States and only to those who have not blocked 900 services. The number is 1-900-446-6075 extension 835 ("TEK") and the cost is $2.95 per minute. The other method is to bill the call to a credit card at $2.95 per minute. For this option, call +1-408-261-6630 and ask for the $2.95 per minute technical support. We will attempt to answer any technical questions you may have; although our expertise is concentrated in the Linux area, most of us have experience with other operating systems both on PCs and on workstations. This is also the technical support option to use if you wish to be walked through an installation. This service is available M-F 11 am-5 pm pacific time, although you may try calling at any time as our technicians are often in late working on a project.

8.5.2 Guaranteed Technical Support

At Yggdrasil, we also offer guaranteed technical support for $25.00 for one question which should take at most 15 minutes. If your problem is not solved, then you are not charged. For this option call toll free +1-800-261-6630 or +1-408-261-6630 and ask for guaranteed technical support. The $25.00 will be billed to your credit card. This service is good for single questions that you believe will take more than 5 minutes but not more than 15. We also accept email (tech-support@yggdrasil.com) and fax (+1-408-261-6631) requests for technical support on this type of service.

The serial number on the inside back cover the this manual entitles you to one free use of our $25 Guaranteed Technical Support service (capped at 15 minutes), and $5 off of your second call. If your the call does not answer a question or solve a problem, your free call or $5 discount is still valid for your next call.

8.5.3 Personal Technical Support Contract

For those individuals needing more in-depth support than either of the above options provides, we also offer a 1 year or 1 engineering hour personal technical support contract for $100. The contract is renewable at the rate of $100 per hour and expires after 1 year. This contract is good for such services as coding, supplying newer versions of programs, or answering questions of any length. Clearly this is the best option for anyone who has 4 or more questions which will take more than 30 minutes to answer, or who needs support which requires updated programs or in-depth analysis.

8.5.4 Business Technical Support Contract

With this support contract, Yggdrasil will fix Plug and Play Linux bugs and implement temporary workarounds as necessary to minimize downtime due to Plug and Play Linux problems. Traditional support prices are quoted individually, generally in units of one year, and are loosely based on the formula

$$(\text{machines} + \text{contactpeople} + \text{users}) \times \$60/month$$

For example, a single-user machine would work out to about $180/month or $1260/year.

8.5.5 Release on Demand

For $500, Yggdrasil will fix the Plug and Play Linux problem of your choice and send you a new gold CD-R with the problem fixed.

8.5.6 General Technical Services

At Yggdrasil, we also do general contracting and development. If you need a new device driver, application, or other miscellaneous project, we will do the development at a rate of $300/hour plus the cost of any special hardware or software required by the project. All software developed at Yggdrasil Computing under this service will be covered by either the GNU General Public License or the GNU Library General Public License.

8.5.7 Fixed Price Development Contracts

At your request Yggdrasil will submit a bid for software development projects starting at $5,000. Fixed price bids are computed on the basis of $400 per estimated engineering hour.

9 PC Hardware

In many ways, PC hardware is not the best choice for a multi-tasking operating system. Much of the older hardware available on the market has only been tested in a single-tasking system and fails under the additional load which occurs in multi-tasking environments. That being said, the price/performance ratio of PC hardware is currently the best available; even NASA is looking into replacing supercomputers with multiple PC's working together.

To complicate matters, there are several PC buses to contend with.

9.1 The ISA Bus

The Industry Standard Architecture (ISA) bus is an extension and standardization of the bus that appeared in the original IBM PCXTs and IBM PCATs. It suffers from many problems, not the least of which is its inability to share interrupts or to provide configuration information to any of the cards plugged into it. This is the bus that most PC users are familiar with; it requires setting dip switches and changing jumpers. Hardware for the ISA bus is generally inexpensive but relatively slow.

The biggest drawback of the ISA bus is its inability to share interrupts. Under a single-tasking operating system such as DOS, this is not a problem since many drivers use busy wait loops instead of interrupts and DOS even assigns COM1 and COM3 to the same IRQ; however Linux does use interrupts and such a setup will fail under Linux. Furthermore it is possible that *sharing interrupts on the ISA bus can damage your hardware.* Many problems people have with Linux stem from interrupt conflicts.

9.2 The EISA Bus

The Extended Industry Standard Architecture (EISA) bus is an extension of the ISA bus which allows for software configuration, shared interrupts, and faster data transfer rates. The EISA bus has never had the popularity that the ISA bus had and EISA cards are usually much more expensive than their ISA counterparts. Furthermore, special configuration software is usually required to configure the machines, and such software does not run under Linux.

9.3 The PCI Bus

The latest bus to enter the PC market, and the one that currently appears to be the wave of the future, is the PCI Bus. It was designed to need no configuration and to be completely processor independent. Sadly, neither of these goals has been met. With early PCI motherboards, it was not uncommon to have to set jumpers on add-in boards and the motherboard, and also to set configuration information in the CMOS. With current PCI motherboards it is usually enough to change the CMOS settings to get a new add-in board to work. The PCI bus is supposed to allow the sharing of interrupts; because of ISA bus considerations, this is rarely implemented, however.

9.4 The VESA Bus

The Video Equipment Standards Organization (VESA) established a Local Bus to speed video throughput on PCs. From the point of view of a Linux user, this is just a fast ISA bus with all of its related problems.

9.5 The PCMCIA Bus

Many laptops have a PCMCIA bus which allows hot swapping and other features. David Hinds has added support for many PCMCIA cards into Linux. Currently this requires a daemon to be run at boot time as well as several modules to be loaded. Please see the PCMCIA howto for information on setting up a PCMCIA bus.

9.6 The MCA Bus

IBM created the micro channel architecture (MCA) bus as a failed attempt to regain control of the PC world. The result was an expensive, proprietary bus which did not catch on. There is almost no support for the MCA bus in Linux. Check the FTP sites for drivers for a few MCA systems.

10 Linux Specific Items

Most users and administrators of other un*x clones should have no problems with Linux. There are, however, a few commands which are unique to Linux. This chapter attempts to mention the major Linux specific commands and how to use them.

10.1 Keymaps

Since Linux is an operating system of international character, it must support many different keyboards. The command that tells the kernel which keyboard you are using is `loadkeys`. In general you should never need to use this command under Plug and Play Linux because the install script asks you which keyboard type you have and creates the file '`/etc/rc.d/rc.misc/rc.kbd`' to set the keyboard type every time you reboot. However, if you wish to create a custom keymap, then you will need to use loadkeys to load it. Type

```
man loadkeys
```

for information on how to use loadkeys, and type

```
man keytables
```

for information on creating your own custom keymaps.

10.2 Video Modes

Many PC video cards support several text modes, not just 80 characters by 24 lines. Under Linux, the only normal way to select a video mode is during the boot sequence or with LILO (See Section 4.1.1 [Booting with LILO], page 30.) There is some experimental software included on one of the FTP site dumps which will allow you to change video modes on the fly, but it requires quite a bit of work to install.

11 Setting Up Serial Ports

On PCs, it is possible to locate serial ports nearly anywhere in the I/O space, and since there is a limit of one card per interrupt, creative allocation of interrupts is usually required to get more than 2 serial ports onto a single machine. The program `setserial` is used to tell the kernel the location of the serial ports. For information on how to use the `setserial` program, type

```
man setserial
```

12 Changing Console Settings

The Linux console supports some non-standard features which can be controlled through the program `setterm`. Type

```
man setterm
```

for information on how to use this utility.

12.1 Setting Hard Driver Parameters

Linux allows the hard driver parameters to be set for better through put on some systems. Many EIDE drives include special features which are not quite standard, or do not work correctly on all controllers. The program **hdparm** allows these parameters to be tuned. For more information on **hdparm** type

```
man hdparm
```

12.2 kbdrate

The keyboard repeat rate is setable on most PC keyboards. The kbdrate program allows both the rate and delay time to be set. Type

```
man kbdrate
```

for more information on `kbdrate`.

12.3 tunelp

Since many PC parallel ports do not use interrupts correctly, Linux defaults to using a polling parallel port driver. To tune your port for maximum efficiency, or if you wish to turn on parallel port interrupts, use the command `tunelp`. For information on the `tunelp` command, type

```
man tunelp
```

13 Device Special Files

Under Linux device drivers and the devices they control are accessed via device special files usually located in the directory '/dev'. Running `ls -l` on '/dev' will list out important information about each device. For example

```
# ls -l /dev/tty*
crw-rw-rw- 1 root system 5, 0 Aug 18 1994 /dev/tty
crw-rw-rw- 1 root other 4, 1 Jun 1 01:03 /dev/tty1
crw-rw-rw- 1 root other 4, 2 May 31 23:45 /dev/tty2
crw-rw-rw- 1 root other 4, 3 May 31 23:45 /dev/tty3
crw-rw-rw- 1 root other 4, 4 May 31 23:45 /dev/tty4
crw-rw-rw- 1 randy system 4, 5 Dec 7 08:41 /dev/tty5
crw-rw-rw- 1 biro system 4, 6 Dec 7 08:41 /dev/tty6
crw-rw-rw- 1 root other 19, 32 Jun 1 08:46 /dev/ttyC0
crw-rw-rw- 1 root other 19, 33 May 31 23:45 /dev/ttyC1
crw-rw-rw- 1 root other 19, 34 May 31 23:45 /dev/ttyC2
crw-rw-rw- 1 root other 19, 35 Jun 1 12:02 /dev/ttyC3
crw------- 1 Shpa other 19, 36 May 31 23:46 /dev/ttyC4
crw-rw-rw- 1 root tty 19, 37 Mar 6 20:52 /dev/ttyC5
crw-rw-rw- 1 root tty 19, 38 Mar 6 20:52 /dev/ttyC6
crw-rw-rw- 1 root tty 19, 39 Mar 6 20:52 /dev/ttyC7
crw-rw-rw- 1 uucp system 4, 64 Jul 21 1993 /dev/ttyS0
```

The first four columns of information have basically the same meaning here as for other files. The 'c' as the very first character means that these are device special files for character devices; the fifth and sixth columns contain the major number and minor number of the device respectively. Each device file has a major number and minor number associated with it; the major number indicates which device driver it is associated with, and the minor number is used to determine which device to access when a single driver controls more than one device or specifies any special methods to use to access the device. For example for a floppy device, the minor number determines not only which floppy drive to access, but also whether the floppy is a 5.25 or 3.5 inch drive and whether it is single or double density. Fortunately this is normally hidden from the user by the use of '/dev/fd0', which auto-detects the type and format of the first floppy drive, and '/dev/fd1' which does the same for the second.

See '/usr/doc/device-list/devices.txt' for the definitive list of device special files.

14 File Systems and Mounting

Linux, unlike DOS, has a single root directory which all files sit below; there is no concept of drive letters, but instead one grafts file systems onto the root file system at places called mount points. Mount points can be anywhere that is currently accessible, but must be directories. When a file system is grafted over a directory, the contents of that directory are no longer accessible; instead when you look in the directory, you will see the contents of the mounted file system.

14.1 The Mount Command

The command used to graft a new file system onto an existing one is the `mount` command. In its simplest form, the `mount` command takes two arguments. The first is the device special file (See Chapter 13 [devices], page 88) and the second is the mount point. So to mount a filesystem that is on floppy drive 0, ('`/dev/fd0`') onto '`/mnt`' one would type

```
mount /dev/fd0 /mnt
```

There is nothing special about '`/mnt`', it is just a traditional place to mount additional file systems which are not automatically mounted at boot time. So if the floppy was a Plug and Play boot floppy and it was in the drive when you issued the mount command, typing `ls` would show

```
# mount /dev/fd0 /mnt
# ls /mnt
bin etc lib proc tmp
dev fixes linux ramdisk updates
ekern.gz ldlinux.sys mnt system_cd var
# umount /mnt
```

The files and directories you see here are the ones on the floppy. Under DOS, this would be the equivalent of typing

```
dir a:
```

A word of caution: Linux, like most un*x clones, caches information about the file system. If you do not unmount (See Section 14.5 [umount], page 98.) a file system before turning your machine off or removing a disk from the drive, *you can damage your files.*

Mount has several options which work for any file system type. These include

`-a` mount all the file systems listed in '`/etc/fstab`'.

`-f` Causes mount to do everything but the actual mount operation. Useful for debugging.

`-n` Do not write to '`/etc/mtab`' when mounting.

`-r` The file system should be mounted read only.

`-t <file system type>`
Specify the type of file system to mount.

`-v` Be verbose.

`-w` Mount the file system read-write.

So for example to mount a DOS floppy in the first floppy drive, read only on '`/mnt`' with mount being verbose, one would type

```
mount -t dos -v -r /dev/fd0 /mnt
```

There is one other option to mount which is used to specify many different things. It is the `-o` option,k which is used to specify arbitrary parameters which may be file system dependent. To use `-o` one just follows it with a string. For example

```
mount -t dos -v -o ro /dev/fd0 /mnt
```

has the same effect as the previous example. The following `-o` options are supported by all file systems; however, some only make sense when used in '`/etc/fstab`'. See Section 14.4 [fstab], page 96.

async All I/O to the file system should be done asynchronously.

auto Can be mounted with `-a` option.

defaults Default options: rw, suid, dev, exec, auto, nouser, async.

dev Interpret device special files on the file system.

exec Permit execution of binaries on the file system.

noauto Will not be mounted with the `-a` option.

nodev Do not interpret device special files on the file system.

noexec Do not permit execution of binaries on the file system.

nosuid Do not allow set user id or set group id bits to take effect.

nouser Do not allow a non root user to mount the file system.

remount Attempt to remount the file system, changing some of the options.

ro Mount the file system read only.

rw Mount the file system read write.

suid Allow set user id and set group id bits to take effect.

sync Do all I/O to the file system synchronously.

user Allow an ordinary user to mount the file system. This also adds the following options: noexec, nosuid, nodev, unless explicitly overridden by the superuser.

Sometimes `mount` will fail with an error message '`can't create lock file /etc/mtab~: File exists`'. This is to prevent more than one copy of `mount` or `umount` from writing to '`/etc/mtab`' at the same time; however, sometimes when `mount` or `umount` fails the file '`/etc/mtab~`' is not removed. To fix this, first use `ps -auxw` to make sure that no copies of `mount` or `umount` are running, and then remove the lock file by typing

```
rm /etc/mtab~
```

Once the lock file is gone, mount should succeed.

14.2 File Systems.

Mount also has several other options which are useful under many circumstances. The most common of these is the `-t` option which tells mount what type of file system to attempt to mount. To determine which file systems your particular kernel supports, you can type `cat /proc/filesystems`. One possible output is

```
# cat /proc/filesystems
minix
ext2
umsdos
msdos
nodev proc
nodev nfs
iso-9660
```

For a brief description of all the available file systems, Section 5.1 [Configuring the Kernel], page 35. The "nodev"'s above mean that the *nfs* and *proc* file systems are not associated with a device.

Normally `mount` can automatically identify the file system if it is one of minix, ext, xiafs, or ext2, so you should never need to specify one of these explicitly. Also, the mount that comes with Plug and Play Linux will attempt to mount the file system as an ISO-9660 file system with Rock Ridge extensions if it cannot recognize the file system type and one has not been specified, so you should not need to specify that one explicitly, either. If after trying all these file systems, `mount` has been unable to identify it, it will then try each of the file system types listed in '`/proc/filesystems`' in turn; this can lead to confusion between *umsdos* and *msdos* file systems. It is usually best to specify these file systems explicitly so there is no possibility of confusion.

14.2.1 The *proc* File System

The *proc* file system is used to get information from the kernel about a process or the kernel's state without needing to know anything about internal kernel structures. One example of the information available in the *proc* file system was given above for the file '/proc/filesystems'. The *proc* file system does not actually take any space on the disk even though ls reports that some of the files are quite large.

Commands such as ps and fuser assume that the *proc* file system is mounted on '/proc' to find out information about the different processes running on the machine. The *proc* file system normally contains one directory entry for each process as well as several other informational files and directories. To see what is happening on your machine at this moment:

```
# ls /proc
1 288 55 74 dma modules
109 289 6 84 filesystems net
110 35 63 85 interrupts pci
116 36 70 868 ioports self
117 44 71 87 kcore stat
130 45 72 871 kmsg uptime
139 46 73 875 ksyms version
160 478 732 cpuinfo loadavg
19 5 733 devices meminfo
```

The numbers in the directory listing are process id's for every process on the system. When the ls command was run, there were 34 processes running with process id's ranging from 1 to 875. Each of the numbers is actually a directory which contains information about the process. Since process 1 is always init, the following example should work on every machine.

```
# ls /proc/1
cmdline environ fd mem stat
cwd exe maps root statm
```

Each of these files tells something about the process with pid 1..

'cmdline' The command line used to invoke the process.

'cwd' A symbolic link to the process's current working directory.

'environ' The environment in which the command was invoked.

'exe' A symbolic link to the executable that the process is running.

'fd' A directory with symbolic links to each of the files that the process has open.

'maps' A list of all the memory mapped files in use by the process.

'mem' An image of the process's memory.

'root' A symbolic link to the root directory for the command.

'stat' A list of process statistics.

'statm' A list of process memory statistics.

The other files in '/proc' give information about the state of the kernel and its various subsystems. For example the file '/proc/interrupts' lists the interrupts that the kernel currently is using. This file can be very useful when trying to track down hardware conflicts.

The *proc* file system is normally mounted with the command

```
mount -t proc none /proc
```

However it should never be necessary to run this command as the *proc* file system is automatically mounted on '/proc' at boottime. See Section 14.4 [fstab], page 96.

14.2.2 NFS

The Network File System (NFS) is a method of sharing files between computers which is popular on un*x systems. An NFS file system is mounted the same way as any other file system; however a hostname and path are provided instead of a device special file. The device special file is replaced by the string hostname:path, where hostname is the name of the server, and path To mount the directory '/public' from the NFS server server on the directory '/mnt' one would type

```
mount server:/public /mnt
```

For NFS, mount supports the following options with -o:

rsize=n The block size for reads.

wsize=n The block size for writes.

timeo=n The timeout length.

retrans=n The number of minor retransmits to try.

acregmin=n
The minimum cache time for attributes for a file.

acregmax=n
The maximum cache time for attributes for a file.

acdirmin=n
The minimum cache time for attributes for a directory.

acdirmax=n
The maximum cache time for attributes for a directory.

actimeo=n
: Sets all the ac* values.

retry=n The number of times to try a background NFS mount.

namelen=n
: The maximum length of a filename.

port=n The numeric port for the NFS server.

mountport=n
: The number port for mountd.

mounthost=host
: The host running mountd.

mountprog=n
: An alternate RPC program number for mountd.

mountvers=n
: An alternate RPC version number for mountd.

nfsprog=n An alternate RPC program number for the NFS server.

nfsver=n An alternate RPC version number for the NFS server.

bg If the first NFS mount fails, retry in the background.

fg If the first NFS mount fails, fail immediately.

soft Fail on major timeouts.

hard Retry on major timeouts.

intr Allow signals during major timeouts.

posix Use POSIX semantics for the NFS file system.

nocto Do not retrieve new attributes when creating a file.

noac Disable all forms of attribute cacheing.

tcp Use TCP for communications rather than UDP.

UDP Use UDP for communications.

Many of the options also allow a prefix of "no" to invert them. For example `nointr` is also a mount option.

If you are mounting a file system from an unreliable server, or one which is slow or far away, it is usually advisable to use the `soft` option so that if there is a problem with the server, your machine will not lock up waiting for it to come back up. So to mount the Yggdrasil FTP server on '`/ygg`' one would type

```
mount -ro -o soft ftp.yggdrasil.com:/home/ftp /ygg
```

Of course this example assumes that the directory '`/ygg`' has already been created with `mkdir` and that nothing is currently mounted on it.

14.2.3 The MSDOS File System

The MSDOS file system allows one to read and write files to *uncompressed* DOS partitions. Currently there is no support for compressed DOS file systems under Linux; however, you may be able to access them using DOSEMU. The MSDOS file system supports the following `-o` options.

check=relaxed
: Case is ignored in file names, and long file names are truncated to 8.3.

check=normal
: Like `check=relaxed` but special characters are rejected.

check=strict
: Like `check=normal` but names may not contain long parts.

conv=binary
: No translation on the files is performed.

conv=text
: Carriage return, line feed pairs are translated to newlines.

conv=auto
: `conv=text` translation is performed unless the file has a "well-known binary" extension.

debug
: Causes mount to print out some debugging information.

fat=value
: Allows one to specify the FAT size rather than letting the kernel autodetect it.

gid=value
: Set the group id of all files in the file system to value.

quiet
: Causes commands which don't make sense in the MSDOS file system, such as chown or chmod to not return strange errors, although they still fail.

uid=value
: Set the user id of all files in the system to value.

umask=value
: Give every file in the file system a umask of value.

So to mount the first partition on the first (E)IDE drive on '`/dos`' as an MSDOS file system, giving everyone read and write permissions, one would type

```
mount -t msdos -o umask=0 /dev/hda1 /dos
```

There are other file systems available under Linux, each with its own options; however these three should be enough for most uses, and information about other file systems may be obtained by typing

```
man mount
```

14.3 The mtab file

Perhaps the most important file which mount uses is the file '/etc/mtab'. This file is where mount and umount keep a record of which devices are mounted, and where they are mounted. A sample mtab file is

```
# cat /etc/mtab
/dev/sda1 / ext2 rw 0 0
/dev/sda3 /a/asgard/home2 ext2 rw 0 0
/dev/sda4 /a/asgard/home ext2 rw 0 0
/proc /proc proc rw 0 0
```

The first 4 fields of the mtab file are all you should ever have to worry about. The first field is the name of the device special file. The second field is the mount point, the third field is the file system type and the fourth specifies whether the file system is mounted read-only or read-write.

Under normal use, a user or system administrator should not need to be concerned with the mtab file. The normal way to get a list of mounted file systems is to use the mount command. The mount command with no arguments lists the currently mounted file systems. For example

```
# mount
/dev/sda1 on / type ext2 (rw)
/dev/sda3 on /a/asgard/home2 type ext2 (rw)
/dev/sda4 on /a/asgard/home type ext2 (rw)
/proc on /proc type proc (rw)
```

In the event that '/etc/mtab' becomes corrupted, complete recovery is difficult. Usually the best course of action is to reboot the system, which should rebuild '/etc/mtab'.

The other problem that occurs with '/etc/mtab' is that mount will sometimes leave the lock file '/etc/mtab~' in place, and then subsequent attempts to mount or unmount a file system will fail. The solution to this is to verify that no other copies of mount or umount are running with the ps -auxw command, and then type

```
rm /etc/mtab~
```

14.4 The fstab file

When Linux first boots, only the root file system is mounted. Usually there are other file systems, such as '/proc', which need to be mounted before the system can function normally. A list of all such file systems is kept in the file '/etc/fstab'. This file is also used by programs such as fsck and dump to see what file systems they should work on, so the root partition should also be listed. A sample fstab file is

```
# cat /etc/fstab
# /etc/fstab
# static file system information
#
# This file is not used by the kernel, but rather by mount(8) and umount(8)
# Comment lines have "#" in the first column. Entries that are to be
# ignored should have "none" in the directory field, and have type "ignore"
# or options "xx". Frequency and pass are numeric
# fields for dump(8) and fsck(8).

# device directory type options freq pass
/dev/sda1 / ext2 defaults 0 1
/dev/sda2 none swap sw 0 0
/dev/sda3 /a/asgard/home2 ext2 defaults 0 2
/dev/sda4 /a/asgard/home ext2 defaults 0 2
/proc /proc proc defaults 0 2
```

Lines which begin with a '#', and blank lines, are ignored. The first column lists the device special file, the second tells where it should be mounted, the third tells the file system type, and the forth gives the options. The last two columns are used by **dump** and **fsck** respectively. The options field lists the options for **mount** (See Section 14.1 [mount], page 89.). At boot time the equivalent of

```
mount device directory -t type -o options
```

is executed, so the third entry in the table would cause something equivalent to

```
mount /dev/sda3 /a/asgard/home2 -t ext2 -o defaults
```

to be executed when Linux is first booted.

Notice that the line

```
/dev/sda2 none swap sw 0 0
```

would generate the mount command

```
mount /dev/sda2 none -t swap -o sw
```

which should return the error message

```
mount: fs type swap not supported by kernel
```

This line is actually used to specify the swap device and will cause the equivalent of

```
swapon /dev/sda2
```

to be executed at boot time. See Chapter 15 [swap], page 100.

The fstab file is also useful when combined with the **noauto** option. If there is a file system you mount often, but not all the time, then it can be put into '/etc/fstab' with the **noauto** option and it can then be mounted by specifying only the device special file or the mount point. For example if the line

```
/dev/cdrom /system_cd iso-9660 noauto 0 1
```

is in '/etc/fstab' then a CD-ROM can be mounted on '/system_cd' by typing either

```
mount /system_cd
```

or

```
mount /dev/cdrom
```

Another useful feature of the fstab file is to allow users to mount their own file systems while limiting the accompanying security risks. The **user** option in '/etc/fstab' allows this and helps to minimize security risks. For example if the line

```
/dev/fd0 /floppy msdos user 0 0
```

is in '/etc/fstab' and the directory '/floppy' exists a user will be able to mount and unmount floppies on '/floppy' with the command

```
mount /floppy
```

and

```
umount /floppy
```

In this way users can import files without intervention by the system administrator, and without opening large security holes.

14.5 Unmounting File Systems

As mentioned earlier, mounted file systems must be unmounted before the disk is removed from the drive or the system is turned off. Failure to do so can lead to *loss of data*. Unmounting a file system is accomplished with the **umount** command. The argument to **umount** is either the device special file, or the mount point. So if '/dev/cdrom' is mounted on '/system_cd' then either of the commands

```
umount /dev/cdrom
```

or

```
umount /system_cd
```

will unmount '/system_cd' if nothing is currently using '/system_cd'. If **umount** returns the error message

```
# umount /system_cd
umount: /dev/cdrom: device is busy
```

or something similar it means that '/system_cd' is in use. This can be a process which has an open file somewhere beneath '/system_cd' or another file system which is mounted beneath '/system_cd'. The only way to unmount such a file system is to kill all the processes which are using

'`/system_cd`' and then unmount all the file systems which are mounted on it. Plug and Play Linux comes with a special program, `fumount` which uses `fuser` and '`/etc/mtab`' to attempt to accomplish this for you. Type

```
man fumount
```

for more information on this command. The command

```
fumount -k 9 /system_cd
```

will immediately kill all the processes that are using the CD-ROM, without giving them a chance to exit gracefully, and then run `umount /system_cd`. Because of the way Linux works it is impossible to guarantee that this will succeed, but `fumount` will work in most circumstances.

14.6 Making and Repairing File Systems.

Under Linux, new file systems are created with the command `mkfs`. The command

```
mkfs -t ext2 /dev/fd0
```

creates a new ext2 file system on the formatted floppy (use the program `fdformat`) to format the floppy in the first floppy drive. All data that was on the floppy *will be lost.*

Whenever there is a power failure or other system crash, there is a potential for file system damage. The program `fsck` exists to check file systems for damage, and repair as much of the damage as possible. After a crash and after every few reboots, `fsck` will automatically be run on the file systems which are mounted at boot time to check for damage and repair as much as possible, so you should only need to manually run `fsck` on those file systems which are not normally mounted, such as floppies.

15 Setting up Swap Space

15.1 Swap Partitions

If you want to use a swap partition for virtual RAM, you must first prepare it for use. The command to create a swap partition is **mkswap partition** where partition is the name of the partition. For example,

```
mkswap /dev/hda3
```

would create a swap partition on /dev/hda3.

After creating the swap partition, you must enable it for use by the system. You use the command **swapon partition** to enable the swap partition. For example,

```
swapon /dev/hda3
```

would enable the swap partition in the previous example.

If you want the system to automatically load the swap partition at boot time, you can add an entry to the /etc/fstab file. For example, you would add a line similar to this:

```
/dev/hda2 none swap sw
```

15.2 Swap Files

If you do not want to use a separate partition for swap, you can use a file. You must already have Linux up and running to be able to do this. You use the following commands to set up a swap file:

```
dd if=/dev/zero of=/swap bs=1024 count=8208 mkswap /swap
/etc/sync
swapon /swap
```

The **dd** command creates the file itself. You can replace the count number with the swap file's desired block size. The **mkswap** command will initialize the swap file. The **sync** command will ensure that the file is written to disk. The **swapon** command will enable the swap file for use by the system.

To get rid of the swap file, first use the **swapoff** command. Then you can safely remove the swap file.

16 Common Linux Commands

The following is a reference intended to get you started once you have Linux installed. Since Linux is UNIX, you can also benefit by learning from any of the many fine introductory UNIX manuals that are available.

16.1 Logging into and out of a Linux System

All users on UNIX are assigned their own usernames. When they log onto the system, they are placed in a HOME directory, which is a portion of the disk space reserved just for them. NOTE: UNIX is case sensitive. Upper and lower case characters are treated as different.

First you should see the Login: prompt. Enter your username. For example:

```
Login: randy
```

UNIX will ask for your password next. Type your allocated password. Note that the password is not displayed on the screen as you enter it.

```
Password:
```

UNIX checks the username and password you typed, and if correct, will run the shell program for you. The shell program is your interface to the system.

To log out of a session, you can type exit or logout.

16.2 Shutting Down

You need to shut down properly. If you don't, you can lose information and damage your file system. To shut down, you need to be logged in as root and do one of the following:

- `halt`
- `reboot`
- `shutdown`

16.3 Directory Maintenance

UNIX supports hierarchical directory structures. The following commands are commonly used for directory maintenance.

pwd	print working directory
ls	list directory contents
cd	change directory

mkdir make a subdirectory

rmdir remove a subdirectory

16.3.1 pwd (print working directory)

The pwd command displays the pathname of the directory you are in. In UNIX, the hard disk area is divided into directories. The directories are hierarchical, which simplifies the organization of the files on the system. The topmost directory in UNIX is called root, and contains a number of subdirectories grouped according to function. For example, the root directory contains

bin system binary executables.

boot file for UNIX boot code.

dev file names for system devices, terminals, disks etc.

dos file for code that boots DOS from a DOS partition.

etc system administration files and tools, system scripts.

lib library routines

mnt empty directory used for mounting temporary file systems.

usr application and system specific information.

There are many subdirectories under root.

When you use the ls command to list the files in a directory, those entries which are subdirectories are preceded with a 'd' character. The sample screen below shows this.

```
$ ls -la

total 2
drwxr-xr-x 3 randy system 1024 May 16 12:05 .
drwxr-xr-x 46 randy system 2048 May 16 16:46 ..
-rw-r--r-- 1 randy system 224 May 16 11:08 .bashrc
```

. the current directory

.. the parent directory (upwards towards /)

16.3.2 ls (list files)

This command is similar to DIR in DOS; it displays a list of all the files in the directory. Just like DOS, UNIX systems support hidden files. UNIX systems extend the power of commands by using special flags or switches. Switches are preceded with a - symbol. For example,

```
ls -la
```

The switch l specifies a long listing, and the a switch is for all files, including directories and hidden files. The following is an example listing:

```
-rw-r--r-- 1 randy system 526 May 15 12:15 .bashrc

This is what all this means.
permission settings
| number of links to file
| | owner of file
| | | group
| | | | size of file in bytes
| | | | | date/time of last modification
| | | | | | filename
| | | | | | |
-rw-r--r-- 1 randy system 526 May 15 12:15 .bashrc
drwxrwxr-x 2 randy system 1024 May 17 15:03 bin
```

The first part reveals the permission settings of the files. These have the following meanings:

d	directory
r	read
w	write
x	execute
-	no access
l	link
c	character device
b	block device
s	setuid

There are three sets of permission settings. For example, the first items of the above listings have the following meanings:

```
specifies whether a directory entry or not
| permissions for the owner of the file
| | permissions for group members
| | | permissions for others
| | | |
- rw- --- ---
d rwx rwx r-x
```

16.3.3 cd (change directory)

As in DOS, this command is used to change the current directory. However, using cd by itself will take you back to your HOME directory.

```
cd ..

cd /

cd $HOME
```

16.3.4 mkdir (make directory)

This command makes a sub-directory under the current directory, like the `mdir` command in DOS.

```
mkdir foo
```

16.3.5 rmdir (remove directory)

This command removes (deletes) a sub-directory under the current directory.

```
rmdir foo
```

16.4 File Manipulation

The following UNIX commands are commonly used for file manipulation.

cat concatenate

chmod change file permissions

cp copy

lpr print

mv move or rename

rm remove

16.4.1 cat (concatentate)

This command is used to combine files or for typing files to the screen or standard in. The cat command sends its output to standard out (stdout) ,which is usually the console screen.

```
cat .bashrc
```

lists the contents of the file .bashrc to the screen.

For examples of combining files, see Section 16.7.2 [redirection], page 110.

16.4.2 chmod (change file permissions)

This command is used to change file permissions. Changing file permissions allows you to grant or deny read, write, or execution permission to the user (u), the group (g), others (o), or everyone (a). For example,

```
chmod a+x foo
```

would give execution permission to everyone for file foo.

```
chmod o-w foo
```

would turn off write permission to others for file foo.

Since everything is a file in UNIX (and that includes directories and devices), chmod can also be used to control access to directories.

See Section 16.3.2 [ls], page 102, for more information on file permissions.

16.4.3 cp (copy)

This command stands for copy, and is used for copying one file to another.

```
cp .bashrc tmp
```

This copies the file .bashrc to another called tmp. If tmp had already existed, its previous contents would be erased. Files can also be copied to another directory. The command

```
cp * /usr/tmp
```

copies all the files in the current directory to the directory '`/usr/tmp.`'

16.4.4 lpr (line printer)

This command is used to obtain a hardcopy printout of a file (if a printer is attached to the computer).

```
lpr tmp
```

sends the file tmp to the printer. If you have more than one printer, use the -P switch to select a specific printer.

```
lpr -P fido tmp
```

sends the file tmp to the printer fido.

16.4.5 mv (move)

The mv command is used for moving or renaming files.

```
mv tmp zoo
```

This renames the file tmp to zoo.

```
mv zoo /usr/tmp
```

moves the file zoo into the directory '`/usr/tmp`'.

16.4.6 rm (remove)

The rm command is used for erasing files and directories.

```
rm tmp
```

This removes (deletes) file tmp. Once a file is removed, it cannot be restored. To cover situations where mistakes might occur, a switch (-i) appended to this command will request a Yes or No response before deleting the file.

Some commonly use switches with the rm command:

-f don't ask before removing file

-r remove directory and its contents (can be dangerous)

16.5 Commonly Used Text Editors

UNIX has many popular editors and each is a religion unto itself with many followers. The three mentioned here are:

- emacs
- pico
- vi

16.5.1 emacs (emacs editor)

emacs, a full screen editor, is provided with most versions of UNIX. Emacs is feature rich and it is beyond the scope of this document to describe it in full; to get you started, there is an online tutorial. Some commands used by emacs

Delete character
`CONTROL-D`

Delete line
`CONTROL-K`

Save `CONTROL-X CONTROL-S`

Help `CONTROL-H CONTROL-H`

Info `CONTROL-H I`

Tutorial `CONTROL-H T`

Quit `CONTROL-X CONTROL-C`

Undo `CONTROL-U`

Use the arrow keys to move the cursor around.

The emacs editor is invoked by entering

```
emacs foo.txt
```

This envokes the emacs editor for editing the file '`foo.txt`'.

16.5.2 pico

Provided with Plug-and-Play Linux, pico is a very easy editor to use with on-line help available at the bottom of the screen. Some commands used by `pico`

Delete character
: `<-`

Delete line
: `CONTROL-K`

Save `CONTROL-O`

Quit `CONTROL-X`

Use the arrow keys to move the cursor around.

The pico editor is invoked by entering

```
pico foo.txt
```

This invokes the pico editor for editing the file '`foo.txt`'.

16.5.3 vi

vi is a simple text editor; it has two modes, a command mode (the default mode) and a text entry mode. Some commands used by `vi` (pronounced vee-eye),

Enter text mode insert
: `i` (use ESC to return to command mode)

Delete character
: `x`

Delete line
: `dd`

Save `:w`

Quit `:q`

Abandon `:q!`

Undo `u`

Use the arrow keys to move the cursor around.

The `vi` editor is invoked by entering

```
vi foo.txt
```

This invokes the `vi` editor for editing the file '`foo.txt`'.

16.6 Other Common Linux Commands

cal (calendar)
This command displays a calendar on the screen.

diff (difference)
This command compares two text files, and displays differences between them. There are many different switches and options that affect the output formats.

```
diff file1 file2
```

head

This is used to view the first few lines of a file. It accepts a switch specifying the number of lines to view. The command

```
head -2 tmp
```

lists the first 2 lines of file '`tmp`' to standard out.

grep The grep command searches a file for a pattern.

```
grep change tmp
```

searches the file tmp in the current directory for the text string "change". Using the * wildcard specifies all files. The string looked for can also be a regular expression.

Commonly used switches with grep

-i ignore case

-l list only the filenames of the files in which the string is found

-n display in which line the string is found

mesg (message)
This command permits or denies messages invoked using write. The switches it uses are -y and -n

passwd (password)
All users in UNIX are assigned a password. It can be changed using the passwd utility. The user types the command

```
passwd
```

The passwd command asks for the new password twice. This insures against a typing mistake. The user types in the new password twice. Note that, for security reasons, the password will not be displayed on the screen.The new password then goes into effect.

ps (process status)
This command reports on the active processes being run.

sleep This command suspends execution for a specified time interval, expressed in seconds.

sort The sort command sorts lines of input from files and writes the result on the standard output.

tail This is used to view the last few lines of a file. It accepts a switch specifying the number of lines to view. The command

```
tail -2 tmp
```

would list the last 2 lines of the file '`tmp`' to standard out.

time This command times how long it takes to execute a given command. Type the command,

```
time ls -la
```

The command responds with the elapsed time during the command, the time spent in the system, and the time spent in execution of the command.

uniq (unique)
This command reads the input file and compares adjacent lines. The second and succeeding copies of repeated lines are removed, and what is left is written to the output file. Useful when combined with `sort`.

```
uniq foo
```

wc (word count)
This utility displays a count of the number of characters, words and lines in a file.

```
wc tmp
```

lists the number of lines, words, and characters in the file tmp. The switches for this utility are

-l print line count

-c print character count

-w print word count

who This command displays a list of the users of the system. Using the -u switch displays a list of those users currently logged into the UNIX server.

16.7 The Shell

The shell is a user interface to the system, similiar to '`command.com`' under DOS; it has a number of built-in commands. The shell may also execute a command file (called a shell script).

16.7.1 Piping and Tees

UNIX offers what is known as pipelining. It means that the output of one command is put directly into the input of another command. The | symbol is used for pipelining. A pipe connects two programs together.

```
cat tmp | wc -l
```

This pipes the output of `cat` into the input of `wc`.

UNIX also offers what is known as a tee. This is similar to the cat command as it allows writing a copy to a file to assess correct operation. Also, teeing to '`/dev/tty`' is quite useful.

```
grep randy list | tee tmp | grep foo
```

This splits the output of the first `grep` command, and sends it to the file '`tmp`' as well as to the second `grep` command.

16.7.2 Redirection

In most Linux shells, you can redirect the input and output of commands to other than the standard in (keyboard) and standard out (console). The following symbols are commonly used for redirection:

`<`	input
`>`	output
`>>`	append

For example:

```
cat foo > bar
```

would redirect the output of the cat command to the file bar. In other words, we just made a copy of the file foo. This would have destroyed the contents of the original file bar if it existed.

```
cat foo >> bar
```

would append the results of the cat command to the file bar. The original contents of the file would be untouched.

Since nearly everything in Linux is treated as a file (yes, devices and directories are just special files under Linux), you can do the following:

```
cat foo > /dev/lp1
```

which would send the contents of the file foo to the printer ('`/dev/lp1`').

16.7.3 Background Processing

Another feature of Linux is running processes in the background. When a command is appended with the & symbol, it is run in the background and the shell prompt immediately returns. This is handy for such things as printing documents, as it allows you to continue doing something else instead of waiting for the document to finish printing. Each process in Linux is identified by a process identification number (PID). When a background process is started, most shells will print its PID in square brackets. The job's PID is an important number to know, as you may want to shut down a background task. The kill command is used to abort a job; kill accepts the PID of the task to be shut down.

```
kill 9448
```

would kill the process with PID 9448. You can see what the PID of a process is by using the `ps` command.

16.7.4 Bash Job Control

Job control refers to the ability to selectively stop (suspend) the execution of processes and continue (resume) their execution later. A user typically employs this facility via an interactive interface supplied jointly by the system's terminal driver and bash.

The shell associates a job with each pipeline. It keeps a table of currently executing jobs, which may be listed with the jobs command. When bash starts a job asynchronously (in the background), it prints a line that looks like:

[1] 25647

indicating that this job is job number 1 and that the process ID of the last process in the pipeline associated with this job is 25647. All of the processes in a single pipeline are members of the same job. Bash uses the job abstraction as the basis for job control.

If the operating system on which bash is running supports job control, bash allows you to use it. Typing the suspend character (typically ^Z, Control-Z) while a process is running causes that process to be stopped and returns you to bash. Typing the delayed suspend character (typically ^Y, Control-Y) causes the process to be stopped when it attempts to read input from the terminal, and control to be returned to bash. You may then manipulate the state of this job, e.g. using the bg command to continue it in the background, the fg command to continue it in the foreground, or the kill command to kill it. A ^Z takes effect immediately, and has the additional side effect of causing pending output and typeahead to be discarded.

There are a number of ways to refer to a job in the shell. The character % introduces a job name. Job number n may be referred to as %n. A job may also be referred to by using a prefix of the name used to start it, or using a substring that appears in its command line. For example, %ce refers to a stopped ce job. If a prefix matches more than one job, bash reports an error. Using %?ce, on the other hand, refers to any job containing the string ce in its command line. If the substring matches more than one job, bash reports an error. The symbols %% and %+ refer to the shell's notion of the current job, which is the last job stopped while it was in the foreground. The previous job may be referenced using %-. In output pertaining to jobs (e.g., the output of the jobs command), the current job is always flagged with a +, and the previous job with a -.

Simply naming a job can be used to bring it into the foreground: %1 is a synonym for "fg %1", bringing job 1 from the background into the foreground. Similarly, "%1 &" resumes job 1 in the background, equivalent to "bg %1".

The shell learns immediately whenever a job changes state. Normally, bash waits until it is about to print a prompt before reporting changes in a job's status so as to not interrupt any other output. If the -b option to the builtin command is set, bash reports such changes immediately.

If you attempt to exit bash while jobs are stopped, the shell prints a message warning you. You may then use the jobs command to inspect their status. If you do this, or try to exit again immediately, you are not warned again, and the stopped jobs are terminated.

16.7.5 Shell Scripts

Commands can be stored in a file and executed by the shell, similiar to a BAT file in DOS. Using your favorite editor, create a file called myscript with the following lines:

```
#!/bin/sh
ps -aux > processes.txt
cat processes.txt | grep init
rm processes.txt
```

Save the file and exit the editor. Make the file executable by doing the following at the command shell prompt:

```
chmod a+x myscript
```

Now you can use myscript as you would any other command. It will list all the init processes running on your system. Although this is not all that useful, it is an example that shows how you can use scripts to extend the system in response to your needs!

17 Hardware Compatibility

17.1 Hardware Requirements

System RAM: 4MB (8MB without swap partition), CPU: 386 or above, Bus: ISA, EISA, PCI, or localbus.

Disk IDE, EIDE, RLL, MFM, ESDI, SCSI **with supported SCSI controller**. Configurations range from 0 to 1,028 megabytes of disk. Configurations without the source tree that can run without the CD-ROM range from 35 to 300 megabytes. Hard disk can be shared with other operating systems on separate partitions.

Tape SCSI tape **with supported SCSI controller**. **Experimental (i.e., unsupported)** driver for floppy tape.

CD-ROM Sony 531, 535, CDU-31A, SoundBlaster-compatible CD-ROMs, Mitsumi, any SCSI CD-ROM **with supported SCSI controller**, all IDE CD-ROM drives, **Experimental** drivers for any MSCDEX compatible CD-ROM (by booting through DOS).

SCSI Adaptec 154x, and 174x in enhanced mode, Bustek 542B, Future Domain 8xx, or 16xx, other controllers based on the TMC-950 chip, UltraStor. **Experimental** drivers for Trantor, Always in-2000, Adaptec AIC 6260 chip (151x/152x boards), Seagate ST-01/ST02, MediaVision and Creative Labs sound cards, controllers based on the NCR53C810 chipset, and the Adaptec 27xx series.

Video (For X windows.) 640x480 16-colors for any VGA card, 256 colors and resolutions up to 1280x1024 (for sufficiently fast hardware) for the following chipsets: S3 801/805/911/924/928, 8514, Tseng ET3000/ET4000, Oak oti-067/077/087, Western Digital 90c00/90c10/90c30/90c31, Genoa, ATI Mach8/Mach32/Mach64, Trident 8900b/c/cl/cs, Cirrus Logic 5420/5422/5426/62x5, NCR 77c22/77c22e, or Compaq AVGA. Hercules monochrome. Note: Diamond cards not supported.

Sound Adlib, SoundBlaster, MediaVision, and compatibles. Installable Gravis Ultrasound and MPU-401 drivers are also included. PC speaker is used if sound card is not present.

Ethernet Novell NE1000/NE2000/NE2100, 3COM 3c501, 3c503, 3c505, 3c509, 3c579, AT1500, AT1700, D-Link DE600 and DE620 pocket adapters and ethernet II, AT-LAN-TEC/RealTek pocket adapter, Artisoft LANtastic AE-2, Alta Combo, Cabletron,

Ansel 3200, Apricot 82596, AT1700, AT1500, Digital DE100, DE200, DE202, DE422 and EtherWORKS, Cabletron E2100, Intel EtherExpress, Zenith Z-Note, Hewlett-Packard 27245, 27247, 27250, J2405A, and PCLAN, Western Digital 8003 and 8013, other 8390-based ethernet cards.

Appendix A Optional Software Components

AnswerGarden$ (124.1 kilobytes)
X windows help program.

ElectricFence (38.3 kilobytes)
Electric Fence is a different kind of malloc() debugger. It uses the virtual memory hardware of your system to detect when software overruns the boundaries of a malloc() buffer. It will also detect any accesses of memory that has been released by free(). Because it uses the VM hardware for detection, Electric Fence stops your program on the first instruction that causes a bounds violation. It's then trivial to use a debugger to display the offending statement.

ImageMagick (2838.5 kilobytes)
ImageMagick is an X11 package for display and interactive manipulation of images. The package includes tools for image conversion, annotation, compositing, animation, and creating montages. ImageMagick can read and write many of the more popular image formats.

NetKitBSD (982.5 kilobytes)
A variety of programs used for networking, including telnet and ftp.

WorkBone (15.7 kilobytes)
A CD player program.

X-devel (8202.6 kilobytes)
Files required to compile programs using the X Windowing System.

Xserver (24872.3 kilobytes)
The display driver for the X windowing system.

Xshared-libs (5222.2 kilobytes)
Shared libraries for the X Windowing System. Required for compiling and running X applications.

a.out (6505.9 kilobytes)
Backward compatibility package for older "a.out" executables. Include C compiler and libraries.

acm (5756.9 kilobytes)
an air combat simulator that runs under the X window system. Up to eight players can engage in simultaneous air combat. Players fly jet aircraft equipped with radar, heat seeking missiles and cannon.

adagio (127.6 kilobytes)
Sound player.

agrep (56.8 kilobytes)
A version of grep with approximate (fuzzy) matching.

amd (189.9 kilobytes)
A daemon that automatically mounts filesystems whenever a file or directory within that filesystem is accessed. Filesystems are automatically unmounted when they appear to have become quiescent.

andrew (39233.8 kilobytes)
The Andrew System, including the ez editor for easy creation and reading of documents with imbedded images, equations, spreadsheets, hypertext links, and many other media types.

appres (9.5 kilobytes)
Prints the resources seen by an application (or subhierarchy of an application). Used for debugging and developing X toolkit programs.

ash-linux (95.8 kilobytes)
A small Bourne shell clone, which many features similar to the System V version of /bin/sh.

at (30.1 kilobytes)
Lets you or users start jobs at a specified time.

aumix (9.0 kilobytes)
audio mixer with a curses text interface.

autoconf (934.0 kilobytes)
A tool for generating configuration scripts, which lets you write more portable programs by detecting slight incompatibilities between different Unix variants.

bash (633.4 kilobytes)
The GNU Bourne Again Shell. A convenient user command line shell; also required by many scripts.

bbgopher (30.9 kilobytes)
The Bare Bones Gopher information-searching client by Mark Moley.

bc (122.0 kilobytes)
A command-line calculator program.

bdflush (9.9 kilobytes)
A program used to keep the disk up to date, in case of malfunction.

bdftopcf (35.6 kilobytes)
A utility program for X11, used to convert fonts from Bitmap Distribution Format (BDF) to Portable Compiled Format (PCF).

beforelight (16.5 kilobytes)
A sample screen saver for the X windowing system.

bin86 (56.8 kilobytes)
Utilities for creating real-mode binaries. Required for recompiling the kernel or LILO, the Linux Loader.

bind (552.0 kilobytes)
Software to run a network name server on Linux.

binutils (1621.8 kilobytes)
Programs such as as and ld used to prepare executable binaries.

bison (312.9 kilobytes)
Bison is a parser generator in the style of yacc(1). It should be upwardly compatible with input files designed for yacc.

bitmap (126.7 kilobytes)
A bitmap editor for X11.

blt (491.0 kilobytes)
Extensions to the Tk graphical extension language for things like bar charts, graphs, and drag-and-drop.

bootp (100.1 kilobytes)
Support for the BOOTP automatic network configuration protocol.

bwnfsd (29.0 kilobytes)
An interface to a network filesystem protocol used on some DOS based computers; can also handle certain other tasks like print spooling.

byacc (65.8 kilobytes)
Berkeley YACC, an LALR(1) parser generator.

capture (138.4 kilobytes)
Capture The Flag, a strategy board game for X11.

cbzone (74.4 kilobytes)
Battlezone, a tank fight simulator game for X11.

cdda2wav (33.8 kilobytes)
cdda2wav works with cdrom drives (eg toshiba 3401, 4101 and 3501) that are capable of reading audio data digitally to the host (cdda). Other drives may have been added as well when you read this.

cdwrite (21.9 kilobytes)
A program to write data onto CD-ROM writers.

checklinks (2.9 kilobytes)
Adjusts symbolic links when packages are installed or deinstalled.

chfn (15.2 kilobytes)
The change finger information program.

control-panel (3493.4 kilobytes)
Tools for easy system configuration.

converters (117.1 kilobytes)
Filters for converting between different file formats of typesetting systems.

cpio (72.2 kilobytes)
Copy in/out, an archiving and backup program.

crock (239.0 kilobytes)
Two player fighting game for X window system.

cron (57.6 kilobytes)
Daemon to execute scheduled commands.

ctwm (1369.5 kilobytes)
Tom's Window Manager extended to support multiple screens. Requires X windows.

cvs (219.3 kilobytes)
The Concurrent Versions System, a front end to RCS (the Revisions Control System); extends revision control to include an entrie directory tree.

dclock (31.5 kilobytes)
Digital clock under X windows.

dejagnu (105.9 kilobytes)
DejaGnu is a framework for testing other programs that provides a single front end for all tests. The framework's flexibility and consistency makes it easy to write tests for any program. DejaGnu comes with 'expect', which runs scripts to conduct dialogs with programs.

demo (745.1 kilobytes)
Demo system for Plug-and-Play Linux.

dialog (7.2 kilobytes)
Displays dialog boxes from shell scripts, in color if the terminal supports it.

dict (407.3 kilobytes)
A dictionary-like word list.

diffutils (247.9 kilobytes)
Extracts differences from text files. Can be used to generate source code patches, or simply to locate changes.

dip (48.6 kilobytes)
Dialup IP, a program to establish SLIP Internet connections via modem.

dlltools (109.0 kilobytes)
Tools to build old-style (a.out) shared libraries.

doc (34818.3 kilobytes)
Online documentation.

dosemu (483.8 kilobytes)
The Linux DOS emulator.

dosfsck (31.7 kilobytes)
A program to check the integrity of DOS filesystems (partitions). Equivalent to the DOS CHKDSK and SCANDISK commands.

dox (65.6 kilobytes)
A simple utility to send an event to an X window, designed to make it easier to write shell scripts that manipulate X windows.

e2fsprogs (26.3 kilobytes)
Utilities for the ext2 filesystem, including mke2fs and e2fsck.

ed (118.3 kilobytes)
ed is a line-oriented text editor. It is occasionally useful in tight spots or emergency situations.

editres (70.3 kilobytes)
A dynamic resource editor for X11.

efax (113.8 kilobytes)
A program to send and receive faxes through a fax modem.

elm (606.3 kilobytes)
A full-screen electronic mail reader.

elvis (171.7 kilobytes)
A clone of the vi text editor.

emacs (32681.8 kilobytes)
Emacs 19.18 from the Free Software Foundation with support for multiple windows and scrollbars under the X window system. Also runs without the window system.

everything (1099540.7 kilobytes)
All software on the Plug-and-Play Linux CD-ROM.

expect (686.7 kilobytes)
Expect is a program that "talks" to other interactive programs according to a script.

f2c (446.1 kilobytes)
A Fortran-to-C converter package. Includes an "f77" program which uses f2c and gcc to form a complete Fortran compiler.

fdformat (6.2 kilobytes)
Format floppy disk media.

file (118.3 kilobytes)
A program to identify the type of data stored in a file.

fileutils (407.5 kilobytes)
chgrp, chown, chmod, cp, dd, ln, ls, mkdir, mknod, mv, rm, rmdir, df, du, install, mkfifo and touch.

finddev (0.0 kilobytes)
Used to locate the physical device a file or directory resides on.

findutils (3386.1 kilobytes)
"find" and related utilities.

flex (261.0 kilobytes)
The GNU free version of lex, the UNIX standard lexical scanner generator.

fresco (7238.1 kilobytes)
New experimental C++ graphics toolkit for X windows.

fsinfo (24.8 kilobytes)
Obtains information about an X11 font server.

fslsfonts (32.0 kilobytes)
Lists the fonts on an X font server.

fsp (258.2 kilobytes)
An alternative to FTP for accessing remote file servers.

fstobdf (29.4 kilobytes)
Downloads an X11 font from a font server to a BDF file.

fvwm (499.2 kilobytes)
A very spiffy virtual window manager for X11, with a 3D look-and-feel.

gawk (575.7 kilobytes)
GNU awk. This is a program that can be used to select particular records in a file and perform operations upon them. This is used in many scripts and programs.

gcc (14883.1 kilobytes)
The GNU ANSI C and C++ compiler and binutils 1.9l.

gdb (1553.7 kilobytes)
The GNU debugger.

getty_ps (208.0 kilobytes)
An enhanced version of getty which supports modem commands; intended for dialin fax and/or data lines.

ghostscript (4408.4 kilobytes)
Ghostscript 2.6.1 patch level 4: A free PostScript clone written by Peter Deutsch of Aladdin Enterprises.

ghostview (154.0 kilobytes)
A front end to Ghostscript that support viewing PostScript documents in an X11 window.

gic (65.3 kilobytes)
Graphics interface to CVS, the Concurrent Version System. Used for maintaining software source trees.

glib (1175.3 kilobytes)
Library and editor for electronic sound synthesizers.

gmod (19.5 kilobytes)
MOD file sound player for Linux and the Gravis Ultrasound card.

gn (150.7 kilobytes)
A gopher and HTTP (World Wide Web native protocol) server.

gnats (734.5 kilobytes)
GNATS, a problem and bug-tracking system from the GNU project.

gnu-calc (3896.8 kilobytes)
Advanced calculator program for the GNU Emacs text editor.

gnuchess (1153.3 kilobytes)
A chess program.

gnugo (28.7 kilobytes)
A Go game program.

gnuplot (533.3 kilobytes)
A 2D and 3D graphing package.

gnushogi (460.2 kilobytes)
A Shogi game program.

grep (181.8 kilobytes)
Print lines matching a pattern. This is used by many programs.

groff (2680.6 kilobytes)
The GNU troff document formatting system. Includes 'troff', 'nroff', 'eqn', 'tbl', 'pic', 'soelim', 'refer', a X11-based ditroff brouwser, and can produce output on a variety of devices. This is required for viewing of manual pages.

gwm (903.1 kilobytes)
X Window System "General Window Manager".

gxditview (71.6 kilobytes)
X11 based viewer for the groff document system.

gzip (122.3 kilobytes)
This is the standard compression utility for Linux systems. It reduces the size of named files using Lempel-Ziv coding (LZ77) and is also able to decompress LZW (used by 'compress'), Huffman coding (used by 'pack'), one file zip archives, and adaptive Huffman coding ('compact').

hdparm (24.6 kilobytes)
A program to read and change the parameters of IDE and ST-506 (MFM/RLL) disk controllers.

hfs (35.7 kilobytes)
Tools for reading the Macintosh HFS.

host (24.3 kilobytes)
Program to speak to the name server. host is intended as a replacement for nslookup.

httpd (72.0 kilobytes)
A simple HTTP daemon for answering WWW file requests.

This is what you need to set up a WWW server on the Internet.

iceauth (20.5 kilobytes)
Authorization program for ICE extensions to X windows.

ico (40.3 kilobytes)
X windows demo program that displays your choice of one of a number of bouncing polyhedrons.

indent (84.1 kilobytes)
Properly indent a C program.

inews (11.0 kilobytes)
inews: Used to post news articles.

init (98.5 kilobytes)
The program init, required to boot the system.

inn (1197.2 kilobytes)
InterNet News, a popular news server.

ismodem (3.2 kilobytes)
ismodem determines if the named device is a modem or not.

ispell (1053.0 kilobytes)
An international spell checker, with an English dictionary.

itcl (147.9 kilobytes)
A set of high level language extensions to the Tcl programming language.

joystick (7.3 kilobytes)
Dynamically loadable kernel module to support the joystick interface.

jpeg (153.7 kilobytes)
Support library for Joint Photographics Experts Group image file format.

kbd (884.4 kilobytes)
Utilities to change the keyboard mapping and screen font.

kterm (6.5 kilobytes)
Version of xterm (X windows terminal interface) that supports Japanese Kanji characters.

lbx (230.1 kilobytes)
Special protocol for running X windows over a low bandwidth serial connection.

ld.so (272.9 kilobytes)
Dynamic loading startup program. This program is mandatory for any system that uses shared libraries.

less (118.5 kilobytes)
A text file viewer; more advanced than "more".

libc (10427.0 kilobytes)
The C language library; required to compile any C program.

libc_s (1525.5 kilobytes)
C library emulator for the Intel Binary Compatibility Standard, Version 2.

libg++ (5400.4 kilobytes)
The C++ language library; required to compile any C++ program.

lilo (45.2 kilobytes)
The Linux Loader; required to boot Linux from the hard disk.

linux (19111.4 kilobytes)
The Linux kernel source.

listres (14.7 kilobytes)
Prints the hierarchy of X toolkit resource names.

listserv (26.1 kilobytes)
Program for automatic maintenance of mailing lists. Allows users to add and remove themselves from lists automatically.

lynx (581.5 kilobytes)
Text (curses) based World wide web browser with forms support.

m4 (184.5 kilobytes)
m4 is the traditional Unix macro processor. It is mostly SVR4 compatible, although it includes some GNU extensions. It is required for GNU autoconf and some X Window System programs.

macvert (160.0 kilobytes)
Convert Macintosh graphics files to something more standard.

magicfilter (21.4 kilobytes)
magicfilter is an extensible and customizable automatic printer filter. It selects an appropriate conversion technique for the input data by seeking for magic numbers, and then utilizing the appropriate conversion utility.

mailx (89.1 kilobytes)
Mail is an "intelligent" mail processing system, which has a command syntax reminiscent of ed(1) with lines replaced by messages. That means that it is your basic, bottom-of-the-line, mail program.

make (468.8 kilobytes)
GNU make utility to maintain groups of programs. This is used by, more or less, all source packages.

man-pages (12915.7 kilobytes)
Base Linux manual pages. (You want this.)

man_db (3376.5 kilobytes)
This is the program used to format and display the on-line manual pages. Most online documentation is in the "man" format.

maze (14.0 kilobytes)
Program that generates a random maze and solves it.

mc (311.9 kilobytes)
Midnight Commander. Interesting text based directory browser.

metamail (277.5 kilobytes)
Metamail is the infrastructure for mailcap-based multimedia mail handling. (Also known as MIME.)

mille (113.8 kilobytes)
Milles Borne card game.

minicom (133.5 kilobytes)
Minicom is a Telix-style terminal program that can be used to dial out on a serial line.

minimal (0.0 kilobytes)
Required /usr directories and links.

mkdosfs-ygg (2.8 kilobytes)
Create an MSDOS filesystem.

mkfontdir (80.1 kilobytes)
A utility required to manipulate X11 font directories.

mkisofs-ygg (75.2 kilobytes)
mkisofs is used to create an ISO-9660 (with or without Rock-Ridge extensions) filesystem.

modules (66.8 kilobytes)
Programs for loading and unloadking dynamically loadable kernel modules.

moxftp (414.5 kilobytes)
Motif front end to FTP. Requires Motif, which is sold separately.

mpeg (105.1 kilobytes)
A viewer for MPEG movies.

mtools (594.4 kilobytes)
Tools for accessing MSDOS filesystems. Alternatively, you can also just mount the filesystems under Linux using filesystem type "msdos."

nas (1226.3 kilobytes)
The Network Audio System. Requires sound support in the kernel.

ncurses (2302.8 kilobytes)
An advanced version of the curses library, which supports color.

nenscript (26.2 kilobytes)
A clone of 'enscript', a pretty-printer for ASCII text files.

net-tools (103.1 kilobytes)
A collection of tools mandatory for any networking setup.

nfs-server (581.7 kilobytes)
The Network File System (NFS) server. Required for sharing files with other systems.

oclock (18.8 kilobytes)
Oval shaped X windows clock.

oleo (372.6 kilobytes)
GNU spreadsheet program. Supports both X windows and character based operation. User interface needs work.

p2c (689.5 kilobytes)
A Pascal-to-C converter. Use in conjunction with the C compiler to compile Pascal programs.

patch (56.0 kilobytes)
A program to merge in source code patches.

pbmplus (2398.6 kilobytes)
A collection of image conversion utilities.

pcmcia-cs (173.0 kilobytes)
Tools for supporting PCMCIA cards in notebook computers.

pcnfsd (6.6 kilobytes)
The PC-NFS server. Used with Sun Microsystems' PC-NFS client software to permit a PC running DOS to access the files and printers on a Linux system.

pdksh (300.3 kilobytes)
A clone of ksh, the Korn Shell.

perl (9354.8 kilobytes)
Practical Extraction and Report Language. Perl is an interpreted language optimized for scanning text files, extracting information from those text files, and printing reports based on that information. It's also excellent for system management tasks.

pico (135.5 kilobytes)
Simple emacs-like text editor, usually used with the pine mail system.

pidentd (18.7 kilobytes)
The identity daemon; allows a remote system to obtain information on which user initiated a connection.

pine (1061.8 kilobytes)
The Pine mail reader.

pixmap (209.7 kilobytes)
Color image editor for icons and other small X windows pixmaps.

postgres (14530.6 kilobytes)
Postgres95 0.02: A remote database system developed by Michael Stonebraker's research group at the University of California, Berkeley.

ppp (133.4 kilobytes)
Support for Point-to-Point internet protocol over a serial link.

pql (272.5 kilobytes)
A simple single-user SQL database. For a more advanced SQL database, use Postgres95.

procps (142.0 kilobytes)
ps, w, and other utilities which give information on the state of the system.

pwdutil (12.5 kilobytes)
adduser and pwdutil programs to maniuplate /etc/passwd. Useful for system administration.

qddb (2626.6 kilobytes)
A database program based on "tuples" rather than the normal relational model.

rclock (9.7 kilobytes)
Robert's (reduced?) X Window System clock. Also acts as a new mail indicator. Very neat.

rcs (445.9 kilobytes)
The Revision Control System, used to maintain various versions of a project under development.

readelf (26.0 kilobytes)
Utility to read and diagnose ELF format binaries.

readline (339.2 kilobytes)
The readline command-line editing library.

readlink (2.6 kilobytes)
Output the contents of a symbolic link.

realpath (2.7 kilobytes)
Display the actual pathname of a file after resolving all symbolic links.

recode (228.8 kilobytes)
'recode' converts files between character sets and usages. This program recognizes nearly 150 different character sets and is able to transliterate between almost any pair.

recommended (188469.8 kilobytes)
A reasonably complete Linux configuration.

reve (249.0 kilobytes)
Othello program for X windows.

rgb (24.8 kilobytes)
Build a color database file for the X windows server.

rstart (47.5 kilobytes)
Wrapper around rsh to run an X windows program remotely.

runtime (16859.9 kilobytes)
A reasonably small Linux configuration.

scripts (5.6 kilobytes)
Utility scripts for developing X windows programs.

sed (72.9 kilobytes)
Stream-oriented editor. This is used by many programs and scripts.

selection (20.7 kilobytes)
A program which lets you use point-and-click on the text console.

sh-utils (362.4 kilobytes)
GNU shell utilities. This is essential.

sharutils (63.1 kilobytes)
Used to create shell archives.

showfont (29.7 kilobytes)
Display information about a font.

sirc (170.1 kilobytes)
A nice text based Internet Relay Chat client.

slang (317.5 kilobytes)
Programming language, used by dosemu.

smail (1560.7 kilobytes)
Smail, a Mail Transfer Agent (MTA). Required to exchange mail with other systems.

smalltalk (617.7 kilobytes)
The Smalltalk programming language.

smproxy (18.7 kilobytes)
Allows programs that do not support X11R6 session management to participate in an X11R6 session.

sndkit (1464.1 kilobytes)
Programs for recording, playing and synthesizing sound with a sound card, or playing sound on a PC speaker. These programs require that you build the kernel with appropriate sound support.

sox (78.6 kilobytes)
Sox is a utility to convert between various sound formats.

spider (60.0 kilobytes)
Variant of the Solitaire card game for X windows.

sspkg (282.9 kilobytes)
Slingshot extensions to the XView graphics toolkit.

strace (82.3 kilobytes)
strace is a C program debugging utility used to trace though the source code.

sup (140.9 kilobytes)
Yet another protocol for disseminating files over the internet. sup has the advantage that the client can initiate the connection and the server does not have to trust the client.

symlinks (6.7 kilobytes)
Symlinks tests the status of symbolic links on the filesystem and checks for bogus symlinks (pointing to nowhere or in circles, etc.).

syslinux (1356.6 kilobytes)
A utility to make Linux bootable floppy disks.

sysvinit (84.0 kilobytes)
System V-like init program for Linux. This is required in order to boot the system.

tar (116.9 kilobytes)
Extract, create, and list tape archives (tar files). This is used in conjunction with gzip for packaging of archives in Linux.

tcl (2524.9 kilobytes)
The TCL scripting language. Generally used with the Tk X11 toolkit.

tclX (23.3 kilobytes)
Adds many features to the Tcl programming language, mostly features that make it easier to interface with unix facilities.

tcp_wrapper (100.1 kilobytes)
A program to control which systems may access certain services provided by this system.

tcsh (426.9 kilobytes)
An enhanced version of csh, the C-shell.

term (2629.6 kilobytes)
Term, a program to support multiple session access without using SLIP or PPP.

tex (12990.7 kilobytes)
The TeX typesetting system and X preview, written by Professor Donald Knuth of Stanford University.

texinfo (760.7 kilobytes)
TeXInfo, a package to develop printed and on-line documentation simultaneously.

textutils (441.2 kilobytes)
GNU text utilities. Basic utilities used in Linux to manipulate text.

tiff (250.7 kilobytes)
Library to support tiff format image files.

time (20.8 kilobytes)
'time' is used to determine the execution time and resource usage of run programs.

timex (72.0 kilobytes)
X windows program to track how much time you're spending on each project.

tk4 (6445.8 kilobytes)
The Tk X11 toolkit. Generally used with the TCL scripting language.

tkWWW (622.9 kilobytes)
World Wide Web browser for X window system. Requires Tcl and Tk.

tkgnats (85.0 kilobytes)
A graphic client for the GNATS bug-tracking system; requires Tcl/Tk.

tkinfo (87.8 kilobytes)
X window system browser for "info" format hypertext files.

tput (72.5 kilobytes)
Tput makes terminal-dependent information available to users or shell applications.

traceroute (20.2 kilobytes)
A program to track down the locations of network problems.

transfig (206.9 kilobytes)
Translates a variety of image formats to and from fig format. Intended primarily to enable conversion to and from TeX.

trn (403.8 kilobytes)
A threaded newsreader.

tset-jv (22.4 kilobytes)
Tset initializes terminals.

twm (1517.9 kilobytes)
Tim's Window Manager, a rather plain but very common window manager for X11.

umsdos_progs (30.1 kilobytes)
Tools for the UMSDOS (Unix over MS-DOS) filesystem.

usermaint (125.8 kilobytes)
Tools for managing user accounts.

util-linux (1432.4 kilobytes)
Various system utilities. (You want this.)

uucp (1371.8 kilobytes)
The Unix-to-Unix Copy modem dialup mail/news/file transferring system.

vacation (20.9 kilobytes)
Lets people know why you are not responding to your mail for the moment.

viewres (30.7 kilobytes)
Display the hierarchy of resource types used by the X toolkit.

vlock (9.1 kilobytes)
Linux virtual console (VC) locking program. This is used to lock a VC while you are away from your terminal.

wavplay (9.6 kilobytes)
Play sound files. You must compile sound into your kernel in order to use this program.

wdiff (40.0 kilobytes)
A front-end to GNU diff for comparing files on a word per word basis. This is useful for comparing two texts in which a few words have been changed and for which paragraphs have been refilled.

wine (1.6 kilobytes)
An MS-Windows emulator for X11. Currently under development; provided for experimental use only.

wu-ftpd (138.7 kilobytes)
The Washington University FTP daemon, an advanced File Transfer Protocol server.

x11perf (148.3 kilobytes)
Tool for measuring the performance of your X server. Used by X server developers.

xancur (214.7 kilobytes)
Animate the root cursor in the X display (i.e., make it change periodically).

xanim (342.3 kilobytes)
X windows animation program.

xaster (42.2 kilobytes)
X windows asteroid program.

xauth (34.2 kilobytes)
Program for managing the X window authentication system, the system intended to succeed xhost.

xbiff (21.8 kilobytes)
Mail notification program for the X Window System.

xblast (153.7 kilobytes)
X windows arcade-style game.

xbmbrowser (31.1 kilobytes)
Program for browsing a directory of image files.

xboard (182.6 kilobytes)
X windows interface for the GNU Chess program.

xbuffy (31.0 kilobytes)
Displays status of multiple mailboxes and newsgroups in an X window.

xcalc (59.0 kilobytes)
Calculator program for the X window system.

xcalendar (67.9 kilobytes)
Display a monthly calendar in an X window.

xclipboard (39.6 kilobytes)
A clipboard that you can cut and paste data to and from.

xclock (24.1 kilobytes)
Displays a clock in an X window. This particular clock was created with "xclock -bg pink -update 1". If you do not provide a "-update" switch, the clock is only updated every minute, so second hand is displayed.

xcmdmenu (18.2 kilobytes)
Display a list of buttons on the X display that invoke common commands.

xcmsdb (25.2 kilobytes)
"Device Color Characterization utility for X Color Management System"

xco (17.6 kilobytes)
Display X11 colors and their names. Much nicer than xcolormap.

xcolorize (7.2 kilobytes)
Start an X windows client with a randomly selected background color.

xcolors (16.3 kilobytes)
Program to display sample of colors in X windows.

xdaliclock (71.8 kilobytes)
An interesting X windows clock program.

xdiary (72.3 kilobytes)
Appointment book and diary program for X windows.

xditview (70.6 kilobytes)
View ditroff files under the X window system.

xdm (152.6 kilobytes)
A session manager that can be used instead of xinit. xdm is normally started by the system at boot time. Under xdm, users log in under the control of an X windows program instead of loging into the console and staring X windows themselves.

xdpyinfo (19.3 kilobytes)
Show information about the X windows server.

xdu (24.0 kilobytes)
Graphically display the output of the du disk usage program under X windows.

xdvi (94.4 kilobytes)
X windows viewer for files in DVI format. DVI is the output format of the TeX typesetting sytem.

xdvorak (5.6 kilobytes)
Change keyboard mapping to dvorak layout under X windows.

xearth (167.2 kilobytes)
Display a map of the Earth in the root window.

xed (49.9 kilobytes)
Simple file editor for the X window system.

xedit (21.3 kilobytes)
Simple file editor for the X window system.

xemacs (40731.6 kilobytes)
X-Emacs (formerly Lucid GNU Emacs). A version of the GNU Emacs text editor that has a superior user inteface, but only runs under X windows.

xev (15.6 kilobytes)
Creates and X window and displays detailed information about X events that that window sees. Used for X development tasks such as debugging X servers.

xeyes (15.7 kilobytes)
Those darned eyes keep following my mouse!!!

xf (4518.4 kilobytes)
XF-2.3 user interface builder for the Tk toolkit and Tcl programming language.

xfd (25.2 kilobytes)
Displays an X windows font.

xfig (637.4 kilobytes)
X windows structured drawing program.

xfm (675.7 kilobytes)
X windows directory browser and program launcher.

xfonts-100dpi (1679.5 kilobytes)
100 dot-per-inch fonts for X windows. Most users do not use these fonts. These fonts are designed for screens with resolutions of approximately 1600x1200, or very small 1280x1024 screens.

xfonts-75dpi (1417.9 kilobytes)
75 dot-per-inch fonts for X-windows. This is the standard size for most X displays. 1600x1200 displays for very small 1280x1024 monitors are closer to 100dpi.

xfonts-misc (5181.4 kilobytes)
Base font collection for X window system. This font collection includes the mandatory "cursor" font.

xfontsel (34.2 kilobytes)
Program for viewing and selecting fonts in the X window system.

xfs (288.1 kilobytes)
The X font server. Run by the system if your machine is a font server for X terminals. If you don't know what this means, then you don't need this program.

xgas (40.6 kilobytes)
X windows gas pressure demonstration program.

xgc (50.7 kilobytes)
Makes "graphics contexts" by adjusting X windows display.

xgopher (248.8 kilobytes)
A Gopher information-search client for X11.

xhost (15.0 kilobytes)
Used for controlling which other machines you are allowing to run X programs on your display.

xieperf (246.6 kilobytes)
Program for profiling the performance of the X server's implementation of the X windows Imagining Extension.

xinit (25.0 kilobytes)
Start a user's X windows session. This program is run by the user from the console, and handles activation of the Xserver and running of the initial xterm process or other commands given in the user's .xinit file, if it exists.

xkeycaps (537.7 kilobytes)
Display the current X window system keyboard mapping on a image of keyboard.

xkill (13.5 kilobytes)
Forcibly terminates an X windows program's connection to the X server.

xlander (20.6 kilobytes)
Lunar lander simulation game.

xlax (16.4 kilobytes)
X windows tool to send keyboard input to multiple windows.

xless (40.9 kilobytes)
Displays contents of a file under X-windows

xli (245.6 kilobytes)
Image viewer for the X window sytem.

xload (16.8 kilobytes)
Show the CPU load of the system in X Windows.

xlogo (15.0 kilobytes)
Displays the x window system logo.

xlsatoms (10.6 kilobytes)
List all of the atoms in use by the X window system server. Used for development and debugging X applications.

xlsclients (11.3 kilobytes)
List the programs that are currently running on the X-windows display.

xlsfonts (18.2 kilobytes)
Lists the fonts available to the X server.

xmag (34.0 kilobytes)
Magnifying glass for examining the displays of other X windows programs.

xmailtool (285.6 kilobytes)
X windows program for reading mail.

xman (68.7 kilobytes)
Display and browse manual pages via an X11 interface.

xmessage (19.9 kilobytes)
Display text in a window (mostly for use by shell scripts).

xmh (150.0 kilobytes)
X windows interface to Mail Handler user program.

xmodmap (32.2 kilobytes)
Used for examining and remapping X windows keyboard mappings.

xpaint (645.8 kilobytes)
An image paint program for X11.

xpipeman (43.0 kilobytes)
An X windows game that appears to have something to do with assembling a pipeline.

xpm (19.1 kilobytes)
Package to support Portable PixMap format image files.

xpool (38.9 kilobytes)
Simulation of the "pool" billiards game under X windows.

xpr (61.4 kilobytes)
Print an X window dump (made with xwd and displayable with xwud) to a printer.

xprop (38.3 kilobytes)
A tool for reading "properties" of X windows. Useful for developing and debugging X programs.

xrdb (30.3 kilobytes)
Loads your X windows defaults into the X server so that they can be accessed by X-windows programs running on other machines that otherwise would not be able to access your .Xdefaults file.

xrefresh (9.7 kilobytes)
Redraws all of the X windows on the display.

xrisk (246.3 kilobytes)
X windows version of "Risk:" a world conquest game that people play before they learn to play Diplomacy.

xrlogin (31.7 kilobytes)
Invoke an X windows terminal from a remote machine on your display.

xrubik (43.1 kilobytes)
Rubik's cube game for X windows.

xrunclient (7.7 kilobytes)
Runs an X client, but does not return until the client has created its first window.

xset (27.9 kilobytes)
Used for setting and reading sundry options for the X windows server, such as beep volume, keyboard repeat rate, and mouse parameters.

xsetroot (17.1 kilobytes)
Sets the background color pattern for your X display.

xshogi (95.9 kilobytes)
X windows interface for shogi: a Japanese chess game.

xsm (95.2 kilobytes)
Session manager for the X window system.

xstdcmap (13.9 kilobytes)
From the xstdcmap manual page:

"[xstdmap] is intended to be run from a user's X startup script to create standard colormap definitions in order to facilitate sharing of scarce colormap resources among clients."

xterm (208.3 kilobytes)
Terminal emulator for X windows. This program runs command shells under X windows. If you are going to run X windows, this program is basically mandatory.

xtetris (38.0 kilobytes)
Clone of the popular "tetris" game for X windows.

xtexcad (193.8 kilobytes)
Simple X-windows drafting program.

xvier (41.1 kilobytes)
A board games, also known as "connect four."

xview (11083.6 kilobytes)
The Xview 3.0 OpenLook C toolkit for the X window system from Sun Microsystems, plus the Slingshot 2.0 extensions and the UIT user interface toolkit. Sun has recently agreed to switch from the OpenLook user interface style to a Motif-like user interface, so this toolkit may disappear in the future.

xwd (18.4 kilobytes)
XWindow Dump. Take any window being displayed under X windows and save an image of it into a file.

xwininfo (29.7 kilobytes)
Returns information about an X window, such as height, width and borderwidth.

xwud (20.6 kilobytes)
XWindow UnDump. Takes an image file made by xwd and displays it in an X window.

xxgdb (80.9 kilobytes)
X11 based display for GDB, the GNU debugger.

ytalk (136.9 kilobytes)
An multi-user UNIX chat program, which is compatible with UNIX talk, supports multiple sessions (more than two people at once), and has several nice features that regular talk lacks.

zlibc (19.1 kilobytes)
A library which allows transparent access to compressed files under certain circumstances.

zmodem (118.8 kilobytes)
Zmodem modem file transfer utility by Chuck Forsberg and Stephen Satchell. This package include "sz" for sending files and "rz" for receiving files.

Appendix B Trouble Shooting

B.1 "Kernel Panic: Unable to Mount Root"

Make sure that you have a supported CD-ROM drive. If you have a SCSI CD-ROM drive, make sure that you have a supported SCSI controller. If you do not have a supported SCSI controller, you might want to buy a cheap 8-bit SCSI controller such as the Future Domain 850 **with BIOS**, which sells for about 60.

If your CD-ROM is not directly supported by Linux, you can use the new MSCDEX drivers as follows. Boot DOS, and mount the CD-ROM under MSCDEX, `cd` to the CD-ROM drive. Then type `runlinux`. These drivers call the MSCDEX device drivers, so they should allow you to use any CD-ROM drive if you have installed its MSCDEX drivers and if you have run Linux from under DOS.

Unfortunately, not all MSCDEX CD-ROM drivers are as well behaved as they should be. If using `runlinux` does not work, and you do have a directly supported CD-ROM drive and a supported controller, proceed to the next section.

B.2 Isolating Hardware-Related Problems

If there is even the slightest chance that your problem is hardware related, please follow the instructions in this section. Even if your system "works fine under DOS", even if you are sure that your system is properly configured, please follow these instructions anyhow.

1. Make sure that the power cables are securely plugged into your peripherals. This has been a common problem.
2. Remove all nonessential hardware. In cases where you cannot boot the system, removing all nonessential hardware means removing everything except the video card and the floppy disk controller.
3. After removing all nonessential hardware try to boot the system. You should eventually get the message "kernel panic unable to mount root" because the boot floppy cannot find a CD-ROM drive.
4. Add the CD-ROM drive and try booting again. The system should come up. If it doesn't, recheck the previous section, entitled "kernel panic: Unable to mount root." Otherwise, make sure that your CD-ROM drive is at a supported IO address.
5. Retry after adding other components until you have determined the one that causes the problem to occur. At this point, carefully check the hardware components for I/O port conflicts, memory address conflicts,

interrupt ("IRQ") conflicts, and DMA channel conflicts. Also make sure that the device is configured as specified in the Hardware Compatibility chapter.

If you have access to a system that is running Linux correctly, then you may also want to try swapping hardware back and forth between the systems to see which hardware component evokes the problem.

B.3 Recording Hardware Problems

If your hardware is properly configured and still has problems, then once you have determined what minimal hardware configuration elicits the problem, record the configuration in as much detail as possible. Try to record the make and model of each card in your computer and its hardware configuration information, such as IRQ, I/O address, memory address, and DMA channel. If you do this before you call to report the problem, there is a better chance that we will be able to reproduce it and fix it in the next release of Plug-and-Play Linux. However, its still important for you to report any bugs that you find, even if you are unable to provide us with the information which can make the bug fixing process more efficient.

B.4 Interrupt and Other Conflicts

If you are experiencing a problem with a device freezing after a few seconds of use, or a device not being recognized, you might have two devices using the same interrupt ("IRQ") line. Collisions can also occur due to conflicts with DMA channels, I/O ports and memory addresses. You may want to make a chart of your PC's hardware configuration to make sure that you do not have any of these conflicts. This will also be helpful if you add more hardware in the future.

B.5 Common SCSI Problems

B.5.1 Bus Timeouts

If you have more than one peripheral on your SCSI bus, and you are getting SCSI timeout errors, it may be the result of your drive not disconnecting from the SCSI bus as quickly as it is supposed to when it receives an "asynchronous disconnect" command.

Asynchronous disconnect allows your computer to tell your CD-ROM to read a sector, and while the CD-ROM is reading the sector, disconnect from the CD-ROM drive and give the hard disk some things to do. Unfortunately, if your CD-ROM drive does not respond to the asynchronous disconnect command as quickly as it is supposed to, the CD-ROM drive clobbers the command that was supposed to go to your hard disk, your computer waits for the hard disk to respond, and eventually times out, since the hard disk never received the command. This was a problem with a number of early SCSI CD-ROM drives, especially the Texel dm3021 and some Texel dm3024's, although a number of other drives allegedly had this problem too. If you own a Texel dm3024, you might want to check with Texel to make sure that your drive's firmware is sufficiently up to date.

If the SCSI timeouts occur while running mkfs and your computer has a turbo switch, you may be able to solve the problem by putting your computer into its slowest mode for the duration of the mkfs.

B.5.2 System Hangs

If your system boots to the point where your SCSI controller is detected and then hangs, or your system runs for a little while and then hangs, you may have a SCSI device that does not correctly handle non-zero logical unit numbers.

In theory, each device on the SCSI bus can have up to eight logical unit numbers or LUNs. These eight devices might, for example, be independently addressable platters on a CD-ROM changer. Most devices only have a single unit, normally unit 0. Unfortunately, some devices lock up when they are queried about their other logical units. Linux has a "black list" of such devices, but that list is far from complete. You can force Linux to address only the first LUN of each SCSI device, by specifying the following argument at boot time:

```
boot: linux max_scsi_luns=1
```

If this solves your problem, please send us the exact values that the SCSI driver prints out for the vendor, product and version of your SCSI device so that we can add the malfunctioning device to the SCSI black list.

B.5.3 Undetected Controller

If you have a supported SCSI controller and Linux fails to detect it, see the next section ("Forcing Hardware Detection").

B.6 Forcing Hardware Detection

Normally, the Linux kernel automatically detects whatever hardware you have. However, there are situations where the kernel cannot reliably check for the existence of certain hardware configurations or where it is both easy and dangerous to incorrectly activate a device driver for a device that is not actually present.

For these situations, you can specify additional options to the lilo "boot: " that direct the kernel's behavior at boot time. You can make lilo add these arguments every time you boot by specifying an "append= " line in '/etc/lilo.conf'. For example:

```
timeout=50
prompt
install = /boot/boot.b
boot= /dev/sda
compact
#delay = 0 # optional, for systems that boot very quickly
vga = normal # force sane state
ramdisk = 0 # paranoia setting
root = current # use "current" root
image = /vmlinux
label = linux
read-only
append="linux tmc8xx=0xCA00,5"
```

B.6.1 BIOS-less SCSI Controllers

You can skip this section if you are not using a Seagate ST0x, Future Domain TMC-8xx, Trantor T128, T128F, T228, or T130, or the Adaptec 151x/152x controller. If you are using one of these controllers that has a BIOS ROM on board and if the controller is successfully detected by the default boot procedure, then you also can skip this section. Note that the TMC-8xx and Seagate controllers are 8-bit controllers; if your Future Domain controller is a 16-bit card, then you have a TMC-16xx controller, and you too should skip this section.

There is one situation where you do need to type something to the '`boot:`' prompt in order to load Plug-and-Play Linux for the first time. When the Linux kernel attempts to detect a SCSI controller that uses the TMC-950 chip, such as the TMC-8xx or the Seagate ST0x, it looks for particular strings in BIOS ROM. If your controller does not have a BIOS ROM, or if it uses a BIOS ROM that does not have one of the strings that Linux expects where Linux expects it, then you need to tell the kernel where your controller is and what interrupt the controller uses. The syntax for providing this information via the boot prompt is as follows (which line you use depends on which controller you have):

```
boot: linux ncr5380=port,interrupt,dma_channel
boot: linux t128=mem_address,interrupt
boot: linux aha152x=port,interrupt,scsi_id,1
boot: linux tmc8xx=mem_address,interrupt
boot: linux st0x=mem_address,interrupt
```

To use the ROMless Trantor T128 controller set to the factory defaults, you would type:

```
boot: linux t128=0xCC000,0
```

For the Trantor T130B, use the generic ncr5380 driver and add 8 to the port number. For example, if your card is set to 0x350 (the default), enter this at the lilo prompt:

```
boot: linux ncr5380=0x358,254,-1
```

An Adaptec 1510 is apparently an Adaptec 1522 without the BIOS ROM, so just use the "aha152x=" syntax to force recognition of an Adaptec 1510. *scsi_id* should be the SCSI id of the controller, normally 7. This procedure should work with other SCSI controllers that use the Adaptec AIC-6260 chip including motherboards that have this chip built in. For example, to use the SCSI version of the Creative Labs SoundBlaster sound card in its default configuration, you would type:

```
boot: linux aha152x=0x340,11,7,1
```

To use the ROMless TMC-850 controller set to the factory defaults, you would type:

```
boot: linux tmc8xx=0xCA00,5
```

B.6.2 Forcing Hard Disk Detection

The following option will force the kernel to recognize and believe that the first IDE, MFM or ESDI disk has the geometry that you specify.

`boot: linux hd=`*cylinders*`,`*heads*`,`*sectors*

B.6.3 Forcing Ethernet Detection

The following option will force the kernel to recognize an ethernet board with the interrupt, I/O port and memory range that you specify.

`boot: linux ether=`*interrupt*`,`*io_port*`,`*mem_start*`,`*mem_end*`,`*interface-name*

interface-name refers to the name of your networking interface. It is the same name that is used by the `route` command. Here are the names used to identify various ethernet cards:

`dl0` D-Link DL600 ethernet card.

`le0` AT1500 and NE2100 cards. Some NE2100 cards must be specified for the kernel at boot time.

`eth0` 8390-compatible cards such as the 3COM 3c503, Western Digital WD80x3, HPLAN cards, and NE-2000 compatibles.

Appendix C What does *Yggdrasil* mean and how do you pronounce it?

The *Y* in *Yggdrasil* is pronounced like a short *i*. All of the vowels are short and the *g*'s are hard. *Yggdrasil* is pronounced "Ig dra sil," and rhymes with "Clearasil." The State of California rejected the name "Yggdrasil Corporation" on the grounds that it was not sufficiently unique, which is why the company is named "Yggdrasil Computing, Incorporated."

Yggdrasil is the name of the world tree in Norse mythology. The roots of Yggdrasil reached into the underworld, and its branches supported the heavens. This symbolism is intended to illustrate the mission of Yggdrasil Computing, Incorporated: to provide infrastructure to support the free software world.

Appendix D Copyrights and Acknowledgments

D.1 University of California Copyright

Some of the software in Plug-and-Play Linux is covered by the following copyright notice:

D.2 The GNU General Public License

Many parts of Plug-and-Play Linux, including this manual are covered by the following license.

GNU GENERAL PUBLIC LICENSE
Version 2, June 1991
Copyright © 1989, 1991 Free Software Foundation, Inc.
675 Mass Ave, Cambridge, MA 02139, USA
Everyone is permitted to copy and distribute verbatim copies
of this license document, but changing it is not allowed.
Preamble

The licenses for most software are designed to take away your freedom to share and change it. By contrast, the GNU General Public License is intended to guarantee your freedom to share and change free software–to make sure the software is free for all its users. This General Public License applies to most of the Free Software Foundation's software and to any other program whose authors commit to using it. (Some other Free Software Foundation software is covered by the GNU Library General Public License instead.) You can apply it to your programs, too.

When we speak of free software, we are referring to freedom, not price. Our General Public Licenses are designed to make sure that you have the freedom to distribute copies of free software (and charge for this service if you wish), that you receive source code or can get it if you want it, that you can change the software or use pieces of it in new free programs; and that you know you can do these things.

To protect your rights, we need to make restrictions that forbid anyone to deny you these rights or to ask you to surrender the rights. These restrictions translate to certain responsibilities for you if you distribute copies of the software, or if you modify it.

For example, if you distribute copies of such a program, whether gratis or for a fee, you must give the recipients all the rights that you have. You must make sure that they, too, receive or can get the source code. And you must show them these terms so they know their rights.

We protect your rights with two steps: (1) copyright the software, and (2) offer you this license which gives you legal permission to copy, distribute and/or modify the software.

Also, for each author's protection and ours, we want to make certain that everyone understands that there is no warranty for this free software. If the software is modified by someone else and passed on, we want its recipients to know that what they have is not the original, so that any problems introduced by others will not reflect on the original authors' reputations.

Finally, any free program is threatened constantly by software patents. We wish to avoid the danger that redistributors of a free program will individually obtain patent licenses, in effect making the program proprietary. To prevent this, we have made it clear that any patent must be licensed for everyone's free use or not licensed at all.

The precise terms and conditions for copying, distribution and modification follow.

GNU GENERAL PUBLIC LICENSE
TERMS AND CONDITIONS FOR COPYING, DISTRIBUTION AND MODIFICATION

0. This License applies to any program or other work which contains a notice placed by the copyright holder saying it may be distributed under the terms of this General Public License. The "Program", below, refers to any such program or work, and a "work based on the Program" means either the Program or any derivative work under copyright law: that is to say, a work containing the Program or a portion of it, either verbatim or with modifications and/or translated into another language. (Hereinafter, translation is included without limitation in the term "modification".) Each licensee is addressed as "you".

Activities other than copying, distribution and modification are not covered by this License; they are outside its scope. The act of running the Program is not restricted, and the output from the Program is covered only if its contents constitute a work based on the Program (independent of having been made by running the Program). Whether that is true depends on what the Program does.

1. You may copy and distribute verbatim copies of the Program's source code as you receive it, in any medium, provided that you conspicuously and appropriately publish on each copy an appropriate copyright notice and disclaimer of warranty; keep intact all the notices that refer to this License and to the absence of any warranty; and give any other recipients of the Program a copy of this License along with the Program.

You may charge a fee for the physical act of transferring a copy, and you may at your option offer warranty protection in exchange for a fee.

2. You may modify your copy or copies of the Program or any portion of it, thus forming a work based on the Program, and copy and distribute such modifications or work under the terms of Section 1 above, provided that you also meet all of these conditions:

a) You must cause the modified files to carry prominent notices stating that you changed the files and the date of any change.

b) You must cause any work that you distribute or publish, that in whole or in part contains or is derived from the Program or any part thereof, to be licensed as a whole at no charge to all third parties under the terms of this License.

c) If the modified program normally reads commands interactively when run, you must cause it, when started running for such interactive use in the most ordinary way, to print or display an announcement including an appropriate copyright notice and a notice that there is no warranty (or else, saying that you provide a warranty) and that users may redistribute the program under these conditions, and telling the user how to view a copy of this License. (Exception: if the Program itself is interactive but does not normally print such an announcement, your work based on the Program is not required to print an announcement.)

These requirements apply to the modified work as a whole. If identifiable sections of that work are not derived from the Program, and can be reasonably considered independent and separate works in themselves, then this License, and its terms, do not apply to those sections when you distribute them as separate works. But when you distribute the same sections as part of a whole which is a work based on the Program, the distribution of the whole must be on the terms of this License, whose permissions for other licensees extend to the entire whole, and thus to each and every part regardless of who wrote it.

Thus, it is not the intent of this section to claim rights or contest your rights to work written entirely by you; rather, the intent is to exercise the right to control the distribution of derivative or collective works based on the Program.

In addition, mere aggregation of another work not based on the Program with the Program (or with a work based on the Program) on a volume of a storage or distribution medium does not bring the other work under the scope of this License.

3. You may copy and distribute the Program (or a work based on it, under Section 2) in object code or executable form under the terms of Sections 1 and 2 above provided that you also do one of the following:

a) Accompany it with the complete corresponding machine-readable source code, which must be distributed under the terms of Sections 1 and 2 above on a medium customarily used for software interchange; or,

b) Accompany it with a written offer, valid for at least three years, to give any third party, for a charge no more than your cost of physically performing source distribution, a complete machine-readable copy of the corresponding source code, to be distributed under the terms of Sections 1 and 2 above on a medium customarily used for software interchange; or,

c) Accompany it with the information you received as to the offer to distribute corresponding source code. (This alternative is allowed only for noncommercial distribution and only if you received the program in object code or executable form with such an offer, in accord with Subsection b above.)

The source code for a work means the preferred form of the work for making modifications to it. For an executable work, complete source code means all the source code for all modules it contains, plus any associated interface definition files, plus the scripts used to control compilation and installation of the executable. However, as a special exception, the source code distributed need not include anything that is normally distributed (in either source or binary form) with the major components (compiler, kernel, and so on) of the operating system on which the executable runs, unless that component itself accompanies the executable.

If distribution of executable or object code is made by offering access to copy from a designated place, then offering equivalent access to copy the source code from the same place counts as distribution of the source code, even though third parties are not compelled to copy the source along with the object code.

4. You may not copy, modify, sublicense, or distribute the Program except as expressly provided under this License. Any attempt otherwise to copy, modify, sublicense or distribute the Program is void, and will automatically terminate your rights under this License. However, parties who have received copies, or rights, from you under this License will not have their licenses terminated so long as such parties remain in full compliance.

5. You are not required to accept this License, since you have not signed it. However, nothing else grants you permission to modify or distribute

the Program or its derivative works. These actions are prohibited by law if you do not accept this License. Therefore, by modifying or distributing the Program (or any work based on the Program), you indicate your acceptance of this License to do so, and all its terms and conditions for copying, distributing or modifying the Program or works based on it.

6. Each time you redistribute the Program (or any work based on the Program), the recipient automatically receives a license from the original licensor to copy, distribute or modify the Program subject to these terms and conditions. You may not impose any further restrictions on the recipients' exercise of the rights granted herein. You are not responsible for enforcing compliance by third parties to this License.

7. If, as a consequence of a court judgment or allegation of patent infringement or for any other reason (not limited to patent issues), conditions are imposed on you (whether by court order, agreement or otherwise) that contradict the conditions of this License, they do not excuse you from the conditions of this License. If you cannot distribute so as to satisfy simultaneously your obligations under this License and any other pertinent obligations, then as a consequence you may not distribute the Program at all. For example, if a patent license would not permit royalty-free redistribution of the Program by all those who receive copies directly or indirectly through you, then the only way you could satisfy both it and this License would be to refrain entirely from distribution of the Program.

If any portion of this section is held invalid or unenforceable under any particular circumstance, the balance of the section is intended to apply and the section as a whole is intended to apply in other circumstances.

It is not the purpose of this section to induce you to infringe any patents or other property right claims or to contest validity of any such claims; this section has the sole purpose of protecting the integrity of the free software distribution system, which is implemented by public license practices. Many people have made generous contributions to the wide range of software distributed through that system in reliance on consistent application of that system; it is up to the author/donor to decide if he or she is willing to distribute software through any other system and a licensee cannot impose that choice.

This section is intended to make thoroughly clear what is believed to be a consequence of the rest of this License.

8. If the distribution and/or use of the Program is restricted in certain countries either by patents or by copyrighted interfaces, the original copyright holder who places the Program under this License may add an explicit geographical distribution limitation excluding those countries, so that distribution is permitted only in or among countries not thus excluded. In such case, this License incorporates the limitation as if written in the body of this License.

9. The Free Software Foundation may publish revised and/or new versions of the General Public License from time to time. Such new versions will be similar in spirit to the present version, but may differ in detail to address new problems or concerns.

Each version is given a distinguishing version number. If the Program specifies a version number of this License which applies to it and "any later version", you have the option of following the terms and conditions either of that version or of any later version published by the Free Software Foundation. If the Program does not specify a version number of this License, you may choose any version ever published by the Free Software Foundation.

10. If you wish to incorporate parts of the Program into other free programs whose distribution conditions are different, write to the author to ask for permission. For software which is copyrighted by the Free Software Foundation, write to the Free Software Foundation; we sometimes make exceptions for this. Our decision will be guided by the two goals of preserving the free status of all derivatives of our free software and of promoting the sharing and reuse of software generally.

NO WARRANTY

11. BECAUSE THE PROGRAM IS LICENSED FREE OF CHARGE, THERE IS NO WARRANTY FOR THE PROGRAM, TO THE EXTENT PERMITTED BY APPLICABLE LAW. EXCEPT WHEN OTHERWISE STATED IN WRITING THE COPYRIGHT HOLDERS AND/OR OTHER PARTIES PROVIDE THE PROGRAM "AS IS" WITHOUT WARRANTY OF ANY KIND, EITHER EXPRESSED OR IMPLIED, INCLUDING, BUT NOT LIMITED TO, THE IMPLIED WARRANTIES OF MERCHANTABILITY AND FITNESS FOR A PARTICULAR PURPOSE. THE ENTIRE RISK AS TO THE QUALITY AND PERFORMANCE OF THE PROGRAM IS WITH YOU. SHOULD THE PROGRAM PROVE DEFECTIVE, YOU ASSUME THE COST OF ALL NECESSARY SERVICING, REPAIR OR CORRECTION.

12. IN NO EVENT UNLESS REQUIRED BY APPLICABLE LAW OR AGREED TO IN WRITING WILL ANY COPYRIGHT HOLDER, OR ANY OTHER PARTY WHO MAY MODIFY AND/OR REDISTRIBUTE THE PROGRAM AS PERMITTED ABOVE, BE LIABLE TO YOU FOR DAMAGES, INCLUDING ANY GENERAL, SPECIAL, INCIDENTAL OR CONSEQUENTIAL DAMAGES ARISING OUT OF THE USE OR INABILITY TO USE THE PROGRAM (INCLUDING BUT NOT LIMITED TO LOSS OF DATA OR DATA BEING RENDERED INACCURATE OR LOSSES SUSTAINED BY YOU OR THIRD PARTIES OR A FAILURE OF THE PROGRAM TO OPERATE WITH ANY OTHER PROGRAMS), EVEN IF SUCH HOLDER OR OTHER PARTY HAS BEEN ADVISED OF THE POSSIBILITY OF SUCH DAMAGES.

END OF TERMS AND CONDITIONS

Appendix: How to Apply These Terms to Your New Programs

If you develop a new program, and you want it to be of the greatest possible use to the public, the best way to achieve this is to make it free software which everyone can redistribute and change under these terms.

To do so, attach the following notices to the program. It is safest to attach them to the start of each source file to most effectively convey the exclusion of warranty; and each file should have at least the "copyright" line and a pointer to where the full notice is found.

<one line to give the program's name and a brief idea of what it does.> Copyright (C) 19yy <name of author>

This program is free software; you can redistribute it and/or modify it under the terms of the GNU General Public License as published by the Free Software Foundation; either version 2 of the License, or (at your option) any later version.

This program is distributed in the hope that it will be useful, but WITHOUT ANY WARRANTY; without even the implied warranty of MERCHANTABILITY or FITNESS FOR A PARTICULAR PURPOSE. See the GNU General Public License for more details.

You should have received a copy of the GNU General Public License along with this program; if not, write to the Free Software Foundation, Inc., 675 Mass Ave, Cambridge, MA 02139, USA.

Also add information on how to contact you by electronic and paper mail.

If the program is interactive, make it output a short notice like this when it starts in an interactive mode:

Gnomovision version 69, Copyright (C) 19yy name of author Gnomovision comes with ABSOLUTELY NO WARRANTY; for details type 'show w'. This is free software, and you are welcome to redistribute it under certain conditions; type 'show c' for details.

The hypothetical commands 'show w' and 'show c' should show the appropriate parts of the General Public License. Of course, the commands you use may be called something other than 'show w' and 'show c'; they could even be mouse-clicks or menu items–whatever suits your program.

You should also get your employer (if you work as a programmer) or your school, if any, to sign a "copyright disclaimer" for the program, if necessary. Here is a sample; alter the names:

Yoyodyne, Inc., hereby disclaims all copyright interest in the program 'Gnomovision' (which makes passes at compilers) written by James Hacker.

<signature of Ty Coon>, 1 April 1989 Ty Coon, President of Vice

This General Public License does not permit incorporating your program into proprietary programs. If your program is a subroutine library, you may consider it more useful to permit linking proprietary applications with the library. If this is what you want to do, use the GNU Library General Public License instead of this License.

D.3 Other Copyrights

Many of the programs in Plug-and-Play Linux are covered by copyrights of the Massachusetts Institute of Technology, Digital Equipment Corporation, Sun Microsystems, and many many other companies and individuals. Yggdrasil is grateful to the many organizations and individuals who have made Plug-and-Play Linux possible, although this paragraph does not imply endorsement by any of those entities.

To the best of our knowledge, Plug-and-Play Linux is comprised entirely of freely redistributable software (with the exception of the locked copy of OSF/Motif) and completely obeys all of the copyright requirements of its constituent software components. If you find any instance where we have included unfree software or are not following the copyright requirements of the software, please notify us so that we can remove that software from the next release or observe the requirements of that software.

Note that much of the software that comprises Plug-and-Play Linux, while free, requires that any derivative works also be freely redistributable. Simply using Plug-and-Play Linux to develop a program does not make it a derivative work of software covered by such restrictions.

Appendix E Third Party Support

In the proprietary software world, an individual or organization that wants to become a technical support vendor can be impeded by lack of access to source code or essentially taxed through source license fees. In contrast, in the free software world, source access is generally available to anyone, and there are no licensing fees that subordinate one company to another, so support services are likely to be available on a more competitive basis.

If you would like to be listed in the next Plug-and-Play Linux manual as a third party support vendor for the Yggdrasil CD-ROM distributions, send a brief synopsis and contact information about your business to:

Yggdrasil Computing, Incorporated
Third Party Support Services
4880 Stevens Creek Blvd., Suite 205
San Jose, California 95129-1034
United States of America
(408)261-6630, fax(408)261-6631
support@yggdrasil.com

The following individuals or organizations are offering support services related to the Yggdrasil Linux/GNU/X distribution.

E.1 ACTCOM - Active Communication Ltd.

14 Pinsker Street
Haifa 32715
Israel

Phone: +972-4-326857
Fax: +972-4-231211
Mail: office@actcom.com

Services:

- Unix and communications consultants
- Internet communications services
- CD-ROM supplier

E.2 Aladdin Enterprises

(name will probably change in the next 2 months)
P.O. box 60264
Palo Alto, CA 94306
voice 415-322-0103
fax 415-322-1734
e-mail ghost@aladdin.com
Contact: L. Peter Deutsch

Background:
Aladdin Enterprises is the developer of Ghostscript and the owner of the Ghostscript copyright.

Services:

- Commercial Ghostscript, including support, upgrades, and alternative licensing.

- Small-scale consulting and contract work in connection with Ghostscript and other PostScript-language-related technology.

E.3 Bitbybit

Kluyverweg 2a
2629 HT Delft
The Netherlands
phone +31 15 682569
fax +31 15 682569
bitbybit@runner.knoware.nl

Background:
Founded in mid-1992. Specialized in Object-Oriented Database Systems. Staff of 6 people. Members of the company have contributed to the Linux Kernel and have ported software to Linux.

Services:
Installation, support, system administration, software development, scheduling systems, database interoperability.

Rates:
DFL 75 - DFL 175 per engineering hour

E.4 ClearVu Technical Writing Services

95 Clearview Drive
Christiansburgh, VA 24073
(703) 382-5697

Contact:
Thomas Dunbar
tdunbar@vtaix.cc.vt.edu

Background:
ClearVu is a technical typesetting company that has expanded into building and installing customized Linux-based typesetting systems.

Services:
Customized systems for in-house typesetting of technical materials using Linux together with TEX and miscellaneous special utilities.

Rates:
Hardware prices vary with market.
Installation and technical support: $30 per hour.

E.5 Complete Computing Solutions of New England, Inc.

31 Syracuse Road
Nashua, NH 03060
(603) 880-0482
fax: 889-6154

Contact:
Burt Janz, President
INTERNET: bjanz@ibm.net, bjanz@ix.netcom.com USENET: decvax!ccsne!bhj
Compuserve 75210,3671

Services:
Custom software design, engineering, and productization; limited custom hardware design and prototyping; consulting; training.

Rates:
$30 to $100 per hour - mutual negotiation and required staff determines final rate.

Background:
CCS New England is staffed by software professionals with over 80 years in accumulated expertise. Custom software produced includes: custom X servers, graphic image converters, cross-platform capable products, network protocol implementations, specialized digital/communications hardware design, etc. Products are typically produced for OEMs.

E.6 Crynwr Software

11 Grant Street
Potsdam, NY 13676
(315) 268-1925
fax (315) 268-9201

Contact:
Russell Nelson
nelson@crynwr.com

Services:
Creation and support of Linux network drivers.

Background:
Crynwr Software has been selling support for free software since 1991. The particular software is entitled the Crynwr Packet Driver Collection (formerly the Clarkson packet driver collection).

E.7 Lasermoon Limited

Lasermoon Ltd
2a Beaconsfield Road
Fareham
Hants
PO16 0QB
United Kingdom

+44 329 826444 voice
+44 329 825936 fax

info@lasermoon.co.uk

Services:

- Networking and comms
- Unix device drivers
- Novell device drivers
- GUI's and embedded systems
- CD-ROM software distribution
- European distributor of the Linux Journal

E.8 LEMIS - Lehey Microcomputer Systems

Schellnhausen 2
W-6324 Feldatal
Germany

Phone: 06637/1488
Fax: 06637/1489
Modem: 06637/1553
Mail: lemis%lemis@germany.eu.net

Modem: The system understands V.22 (bis), V.32 (bis), MNP5 and V.42 (bis). Log in as guest, password Guest.

Services:
LEMIS (Lehey Microcomputer Systems) specialises in system-level support for UNIX and similar operating systems. Services include design and installation consulting, ports, software support, electronic mail connectivity and supply of PC hardware and UNIX-based software. Support contracts are available.

E.9 MB Associates

Domaine de La Grangeasse
05800 Saint-Firmin, FRANCE
+33 9255-2184, voice/fax

Contact:
Michel R. Barthelemy
mb@tsmotel.gatelink.fr.net

Background:
Team with extensive knowledge of system and network design & programming

Services:
System-level support and training for Novell, Linux and other Unix-like operating systems. Customized systems design & production. Design & Installation consulting. E-Mail and networking technologies consulting.

E.10 MCO Zagreb

Hbarska 1B
41000 Zagreb
Croatia
+385 41 612 285
evening modem +385 41 615 556
fax +385 41 533 902

Contact:
Dragomir Milivojevic

Services:
Technical support, custom programming.

Rates:
DM 20 per hour for 1 person
DM 30 per hour for 2 person team

E.11 NeoSoft Corporation

3408 Mangum
Houston, Texas 77092
(713) 684-5969
fax (713) 684-5922

Contact:
Ellyn Mustard
ellyn@neosoft.com

Services:
Custom programming and support for Tcl and Tk.

Rates:
$2500 for a year of commercial support, including 20 hours of consultation, and installation of all new TclX releases during the support period.

Background:
NeoSoft developed and maintains extended tcl (TclX), which is part of the Yggdrasil Plug-and-Play Linux distribution. The company also sells routers and internet connectivity services in Houston, Texas and St. Louis, Missouri.

E.12 Shallow Water Software

PO Box 410
Simpsonville, MD
(410) 997-8584

Contact:
Peter C. Olsen, P.E.

Services:
consulting, systems configuration, system maintenance, and custom software design for small businesses and professionals.

Rates:
$25 - $125 per engineering hour.
Free or discounted support for schools and non-profit organizations.

Background:
Previous work includes the operations research model used by the Coast Guard to measure the amount of work required to clean up the Exxon Valdez oil spill, a draft National Strategy for Civil Aviation Security done for the Secretary of Transportation, now under review by the FAA, and a Community Development Master Plan for Governors Island, New York, among other projects.

E.13 Signum Support AB

Box 2044
S-580 02 Linkoping
SWEDEN

Contact:
info@signum.se
fax: +46 (0)13 214700
phone: +46 (0)13 214600

Services:
Software packages ready to install with telephone/email support and quarterly updates. Regular support contracts. Printed manuals. Installation, modification, misc. support on an hourly rate. Software development projects.

Specialties:
GNU development environment.
Plug-and-Play Linux, Linux.
SunOS 4 and Solaris 2.
Email and news software.
Software for system security.
Software version control: RCS+CVS.
Software for image processing and computer graphics

Background:
Signum Support was founded in 1992 by 6 persons, all with extensive knowledge in system maintenance and systems programming. The company provides support for free software, and does software development based on hourly rates or fixed rates.

Rates
For source code and binaries of single programs, get our free catalog.
Consulting 450 SEK/hour and up.

E.14 Spire Technologies

1439 South West Columbia St.
Portland, OR 97201
Phone: 503-222-3086
Fax: 503-222-5102

Contact: Josuah Drake, spire@teleport.com

Services: Installation, Consulting, Networking, Hardware & Software sales.

Platforms: All x86 models and implementations.

E.15 John B. Thiel

18830 NW Rock Creek Circle #242
Portland, OR 97229
(503) 645-0839
Mail: jbthiel@cse.ogi.edu

Services:
Support, tutoring, design consultation, and custom development on Linux and other free software (device drivers to applications).

Platforms:
Linux, Unix, X-Windows, OS/2, Dos/Windows

Relevant proficiencies:
C, Lisp, i86 asm
Unix system administration
Standard Unix software development tools/methodologies More or less familiar with wide variety of other languages and interfaces, e.g., SQL, Postscript, Perl, Awk, Rexx, etc.

Background:
Computer Science graduate studies (ongoing) Electrical Engineering undergraduate 12 years computer experience; Linux since Aug, 1992.

E.16 The TM Group

P.O. Box 740007
Dallas, TX 75374
Phone: 214-680-1554
Fax: 214-680-2540

Services:
Provide open system training and support

Background:
Founded in 1987, The TM Group provides open systems and client/server training and support in the Dallas/Fort Worth area, as well as the rest of Texas and Oklahoma. Our customers include Northern Telecom, Xerox, and EDS.

E.17 Virtual World Information Systems

(508) 793-9568

Contact:
Lawrence Foard
lfoard@world.std.com

Services:

- Consulting,
- Device driver development,
- Software porting,
- Application development and customization
- Kernel modifications,
- Custom hardware design, including FPGA, PAL and circuit board manufacturing with in-house facilities.

Rates:
$30-$50 per engineering hour.
Fixed price bids available.

E.18 XIS Solutions

Box 1459, SIUE
Edwardsville, IL 62026-1459
(618) 692-2943
fax (618) 692-1420

Contact:
Changyong Cao
changyoc@daisy.siue.edu

XIS (X-related Information Systems) is an employee owned consulting business providing services for the distribution, installation, and support of various information systems. In addition to the support of Linux and XFree, XIS is known to be one of the few which distribute and support GRASS/LINUX – a geographic information system for processing raster and vector based spatial data and remotely sensed images. Our customers include government agencies, universities, small business, and students. Our staff include two Ph.D's in geographic information systems with more than three years of experience managing Sun and Intergraph workstations as well as teaching geographic information system courses.

Our objective is to meet the needs of the rapid development of the geographic information system industry, to provide high quality services at reasonable price, and to facilitate the practical application of Linux and related systems.

Currently XIS provides on-site services (in addition to the mail order service) in the following regions:

St. Louis, MO
New Orleans, LA
Jackson, MS

Appendix F Direct Sales Order Form

YGGDRASIL DIRECT SALES ORDER FORM

SHIP TO: ______________________________

____

____

____

DAYTIME PHONE: _______________

EMAIL: ________________________

Item	Quantity		Price(US$)	
Plug-and-Play Linux (2 CDROM's, 3.5" boot floppy, 140 page manual)	____	X	$39.95 =	$_______
The Linux Bible (1592 pages: kernel hacking, networking, installation, over a dozen "How To" guides, and more!)	____	X	$39.95 =	$_______
Prime Time Freeware for unix	____	X	$59.95 =	$_______
Personal Technical Support (1 year/1 engineering hour)	____	X	$100.00 =	$_______
			SUBTOTAL	$_______
California residents add 7% to help out with sales tax				$_______
Shipping & handling (US: $5, elsewhere: $10)				$_______
			TOTAL	$_______

Payment method: __ payment enclosed __ COD (USA only)
__ credit card (American Express or Optima. Call before using VISA, Mastercard or other credit card.)

Your name as it appears on credit card: ______________________________

Brand of credit card: ________ Card number: _________________________

Signature:_____________________________________ Expiration: ___ / ___

Offers subject to change without notice. All direct sales are returnable for a full refund within 30 days. There is no other warranty for any of this software. This software is provided "As Is" without warranty of any kind, either expressed or implied, including, but not limited to, the implied warranties of MERCHANTABILITY and FITNESS FOR A PARTICULAR PURPOSE.

TAPE EDGES, DO NOT STAPLE

PLACE
STAMP
HERE

LINUX
JOURNAL

PO BOX 85867
SEATTLE WA 98145-1867
USA

What people are saying about *Linux Journal*:

"*Linux Journal* is now a year old. It is an attractively presented publication with lots of color, devoted solely to the Linux operating system. . . *Linux Journal* maintains high quality in writing, editing and layout."

—*Danny Yee*

"*Linux Journal* is the definitive source for getting the inside track on all the latest and greatest developments. The articles are serious and informative, yet lighthearted with a personal touch, making it inviting to both developers and new users."

—*Kim Goldberger*